Inside the Ancient World

ATHENIAN SOCIETY

Jennifer Gibbon

BRISTOL CLASSICAL PRESS

General Editor: Michael Gunningham

Previously published in Great Britain by
Macmillan Education Ltd, 1990
Thomas Nelson and Sons Ltd, 1992

Published in 1996 by Bristol Classical Press
an imprint of
Gerald Duckworth & Co. Ltd
61 Frith Street
London W1V 5TA

Reprinted 1997, 1998

A catalogue record for this book is available
from the British Library

ISBN 1-85399-499-5

Available in the USA and Canada from:
Focus Information Group
PO Box 369
Newburyport
MA 01950

Printed in Great Britain by
Antony Rowe Ltd

Inside the Ancient World

INSIDE THE ANCIENT WORLD
General Editor: M.R.F. Gunningham

The following titles are available in this series:

*Denotes books which are especially suited to GCSE or studies at a comparable 16+ level. The remainder may be useful at that level, but can also be used by students on more advanced courses.

Contents

Acknowledgements

It is no easy task for a practising teacher to find time to compose a book. I am therefore particularly grateful to the following colleagues and friends who have helped with research and advice. I would like to mention especially Bernard McWilliams for the illustrations and James Cressey for checking the references and for many helpful comments. Geoffrey Fallows, Christine Spillane and Margaret Widdess kindly read the manuscript and offered their comments. Finally, I should like to thank my mother for helping to collect material, and to dedicate this book to her.

The author and publishers wish to thank the following for permission to use copyright material.

Penguin Books Ltd for extracts from *The Rise and Fall of Athens: Nine Greek Lives* by Plutarch, translated by Ian Scott-Kilvert, Penguin Classics. Copyright © 1960 Ian Scott-Kilvert; *Lysistrata and Other Plays* by Aristophanes, translated by Alan H. Sommerstein, Penguin Classics. Copyright © 1973 Alan H. Sommerstein; *History of the Peloponnesian War* by Thucydides, translated by Rex Warner, Penguin Classics. Copyright © 1954 Rex Warner; 'The Wasps' from *The Frogs and Other Plays* by Aristophanes, translated by David Barrett, Penguin Classics. Copyright © 1964 David Barrett; 'Antigone' from *The Theban Plays* by Sophocles, translated by E. F. Watling, Penguin Classics. Copyright © 1947 E. F. Watling, renewal copyright by E. F. Watling, 1974; *Hippocratic Writings*, edited by G. E. R. Lloyd, translated by J. Chadwick and W. N. Mann, I. M. Lonie, Penguin Classics. Copyright © 1978 I. M. Lonie, copyright © 1950 J. Chadwick and W. N. Mann; 'Works and Days' by Hesiod from *Hesiod and Theognis*, translated by Dorothea Wender, Penguin Classics. Copyright © 1973 Dorothea Wender; 'The Persians' from *Prometheus Bound and Other Plays* by Aeschylus, translated by Philip Vellacott, Penguin Classics. Copyright © 1961 Philip Vellacott; Society for the Promotion of Hellenic Studies for 'The Ephebic Oath in Fifth-century Athens' translated by P. Siewert, *Journal of Hellenic Studies*, 97 (1977).

Every effort has been made to trace all the copyright holders, but if any have been inadvertently overlooked the publishers will be pleased to make the necessary arrangement at the first opportunity.

Illustrations

Introduction

This book is about the people who lived in the *polis* (city-state) of Athens in the fifth century BC. The *polis* consisted of the countryside of Attica, about 2500 square kilometres containing over a hundred villages, and the city of Athens itself.

The fifth century was a period of great change for the Athenians. It began with unexpected victories over two huge Persian invasions: it ended with defeat by Sparta and her allies in the Peloponnesian War. In the course of the century, Athens gained and lost an empire. Pericles, the leading statesman in Athens from 444 BC until his death in 429 BC, believed that future generations would remember the Athenians for their empire above all:

'Even if we are forced to give way one day (and nothing lasts for ever), yet still it will be remembered that we ruled over more Greek states than any other Greek city ever did.'   [Thucydides, 2.64.3]

Pericles was wrong. Instead, today we remember the Athenians less for their empire than for their achievements in architecture (the Parthenon temple is still one of the most admired buildings in the world), sculpture, painted pottery, drama, history, science, medicine, philosophy and politics.

How do we know about Athenian society?

How far is it possible to enter into the lives of people who lived over two thousand years ago? Historians work through primary evidence, which can be either literary or archaeological. Fortunately, there is a wide range of evidence from fifth century Athens. Of course, it has gaps. All the literature, for example, was written by men of the educated upper classes, and it reflects their views. It is hard, if not impossible, to enter into the minds of women, slaves, foreigners or country people, and yet they formed a vital part of

1

the Athenian *polis*. Moreover, literature can be biased, or simply fail to tell us what we want to know – after all, very little of it was written with the historian in mind. Nevertheless, it is possible, by careful use of the evidence, to build up a reasonably full picture of Athenian life.

Literary evidence

Literary evidence includes anything written and preserved in books – plays, speeches, poems, historical, medical, philosophical and political writing.

Earlier writers can sometimes shed light on the fifth century. Homer's poems, the *Iliad* and *Odyssey*, remained a fundamental part of Athenian education and had a profound influence on thought. Hesiod, a farmer and a poet from Boeotia in central Greece, wrote the *Works and Days*, which gives some rare evidence for agricultural life.

Obviously, the best evidence comes from fifth century sources. Two very different historians were writing at the time. Herodotus wrote a history of the wars against the Persians, and Thucydides a history of the Peloponnesian War. Thucydides will be quoted frequently in this book. He was a superb historian who wrote his work for all time. The speeches which he attributes to Pericles, while not necessarily quite what the statesman actually said, are particularly valuable evidence for Athenian ideas.

Another valuable source are the comedies of Aristophanes. They are set in Athens in his day, and they deal with topical issues and personalities. However, they do not present a realistic picture of everyday life, and although they are often quoted in this book, the views expressed may well be exaggerated and fantastic; they must be treated cautiously. Imagine trying to reconstruct a picture of twentieth century Britain with only 'Spitting Image' for evidence!

The tragedies written by Aeschylus, Sophocles and Euripides are less useful than comedy because their plots are almost always taken from mythology, not everyday life, but they do deal with topical religious and moral issues, and give evidence of the attitudes and tastes of the audience.

Speeches were composed with a mass audience of typical Athenian males in mind. Speech-writers like Antiphon, Lysias and Andocides in the fifth century, and Isocrates, Aeschines and Demosthenes in the fourth, had to appeal to the prejudices of the jury and so they offer much indirect evidence.

The medical writings of Hippocrates and his followers give valuable evidence of the advance of science and often unconsciously reveal male attitudes to women.

In the fourth century, Plato and Xenophon wrote about the life and work of the philosopher Socrates, whom they had both known personally. Their accounts of his conversations provide a great deal of information about Athenian (mainly upper class) life. Xenophon is the author quoted most in this book. He was not a great thinker like Plato, but his interests were wide. He wrote on various subjects, including household management and history. The *Constitution of Athens*, once thought to be by him, is now ascribed to an author known as the 'Old Oligarch' (because of his anti-democratic views). Plato's pupil, the philosopher and scientist Aristotle, also wrote a great deal about Athenian politics. These works cannot always be relied on.

Several later writers are quoted in this book. Two deserve a special mention. Plutarch, who lived in the first century AD, wrote lively but not always accurate accounts of the leading men of Athens, including Pericles, Nicias and Alcibiades. Pausanias, a travel writer of the second century AD, left a good account of the buildings and shrines of Attica as they were in his day.

Archaeological evidence

It was only towards the end of the last century that archaeology became a respected science. Most of the work in Athens and Attica has been done within the last fifty years, and it still continues, with new discoveries being made all the time. Archaeologists build up a picture of the past through material objects.

Inscriptions

Fortunately for historians, the Athenians in about 460 BC started to produce a large number of inscriptions on stone or bronze. Three hundred inscriptions on public affairs survive from between 460 and 400. Most of them deal with foreign affairs – treaties and decrees which show how the Athenian empire was run. The day-to-day work of the committees and treasurers in Athens is recorded, with numerous accounts. Public gravestones were set up to honour those who died for the city (inevitably many men in Athens' constant wars); the laws were inscribed and displayed in central Athens; many inscriptions concern festivals and religious cults; and there are also such things as records of sales, public dedications, grants of citizenship (though these were rare) and boundary stones.

Buildings and their contents

The work of archaeologists, especially the American School, has enabled us to discover a great deal about the Athenians through the layout of their city and the design of their public buildings. Many of the buildings, of course, still stand. These are more likely to be the temples, which were made of marble or limestone, than the private houses, which were made of mud brick. Nevertheless, we have some idea of the conditions in which the Athenians lived at home as well as out of doors.

Objects of clay, stone and metal are more likely to survive than objects made of perishable materials like wood or textiles. Archaeologists have found large quantities of coins (useful for dating purposes), pottery and weapons, but almost no clothing or furniture.

Works of art

The incomplete picture provided by objects can often be supplemented by the evidence from painted pottery. The Athenians exported their pottery widely, and it proved extremely long-lasting. Much of it was found in cemeteries in southern Italy. There are superb collections of Athenian pottery in most of the world's major museums: in England, the best collections are in the British Museum in London and the Ashmolean Museum in Oxford.

The subject matter preferred by pottery painters was either mythology or everyday life. Many of the illustrations in this book are taken from pots. As well as showing something of the Athenians' artistic achievement, they show us hundreds of aspects of ordinary life – women spinning and weaving, boys gathering olives, men enjoying themselves at dinner parties, workmen in their shops, oxen pulling the plough, ships, soldiers, babies.

Although we know that there were some outstanding Athenian painters, like Polygnotos, who painted on flat surfaces, none of their work survives. But we have a great deal of sculpture, from

4

poor quality terracotta statuettes to the superb sculptures which adorned the temples of the Acropolis (see Chapter 2). This was also a period of important development in free-standing statues in marble and bronze.

1

Life in the country

The Athenians tended to play down their reliance on the country-side. It appears little in art, apart from some early statuettes and a few illustrations on pottery. With the exception of Hesiod, Xenophon and a few glimpses in Aristophanes' comedies, writers largely ignored its existence.

Yet the countryside took up much of the time and energy of the Athenians, even those who lived in the city. If they could, they relied for food supplies on the produce of their estates in the country. Pericles was unusual in preferring to use the market:

His practice was to dispose of each year's produce in a single sale, and then to buy in the market each item as it was needed for his daily life and household. [Plutarch, *Pericles* 16.4]

Aristophanes, not very seriously, describes the typical Athenian like this:

a countryman to the core, greedy for beans, quick-tempered, hard to please, not as young as he was. [Aristophanes, *Knights* 41–3]

In the everyday lives of country people, the local village was of more importance – for trading, socialising and religion – than the city of Athens. The aristocrats who had their estates in the area were more influential than the state officials.

When Pericles moved the entire population inside the city walls during the Peloponnesian War, there were cries of anguish:

They were heavy-hearted and unwilling to leave their homes and temples . . . to change their way of life and to leave behind what was, to them, their native city. [Thucydides, 2.16.2]

In one of Aristophanes' comedies, an old farmer called Dikaio-polis is in the city because of the war:

'And all the time my heart's out there in the fields, and I'm pining for peace. I'm fed up with the city and just dying to get back to my village. Ah! my village . . .'   [Aristophanes, *Acharnians* 32–3]

Landscape

Our country is barricaded by high mountains with steep and narrow passes . . . and the interior is also circled with steep mountains.
[Xenophon, *Memorabilia* 3.5.25]

Attica is roughly triangular in shape, cut off from the rest of Greece by mountains on one side and sea on the other two. Most of the land consists of bare limestone hills. There are only three plains of any size.

Plato, writing at the beginning of the fourth century BC, noted that by his day the land had suffered from soil erosion and tree loss:

But in the old days when the land was intact, its mountains were covered with earth . . . and the now rocky plains were covered with rich soil and there were plentiful forests on the mountains.   [Plato, *Critias* 111C]

Plato may have been exaggerating. There were certainly plenty of elms, cypresses and plane trees in his time, but there was not a great deal of good farmland. Of the 2500 square kilometres which make up Attica, only about 500 could be cultivated.

Climate

The rain in Greece falls in winter, between October and May. It can be heavy and lead to floods, but the annual rainfall of Attica, though unpredictable, is lower than that of the rest of Greece. In the 1950s, it varied between 560 mm and 216 mm. In summer, there is often no rain at all for three or four months. When the rainfall was low, the Athenian farmer found his crops severely affected, especially his wheat and vegetables. Crop failures and shortages were a fact of life.

Attica is very hot in summer. In the heatwave of 1987, temperatures reached the 120s Fahrenheit (the 40s Celsius) and several people died. The climate encourages an outdoor life. The skin of women, who stayed indoors, was painted white on pottery, in marked contrast to that of the men.

Farming

The fruits of the earth and products native to our soil are a proof of our temperate climate and the mildness of the seasons, for we have plants which bear crops which will grow nowhere else.

[Xenophon, *Ways and Means* 1.1]

Aristophanes' plays are full of the joys of the countryside and farming:

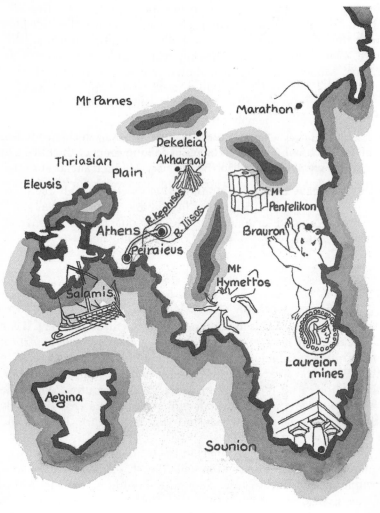

Map of Attica

O Peace, deep in riches, O my pair of oxen, if only I could cease from war, and dig and prune; then bathe and eat my bread and dressed salad, with draughts of new wine.   [Aristophanes, *Farmers* (Dindorf frg. 163)]

O native Attica: hail gleaming land, with fine, rich soil.
                              [Aristophanes, *Farmers* (Dindorf frg. 162)]

You've got everything here – a life of ease on your own small-holding . . . with your very own pair of oxen, where you can hear the sound of bleating flocks and of the grape-juice as it is pressed out into the vat; where you can feed on finches and thrushes.   [Aristophanes, *Islands* (Dindorf 344)]

But this idyllic picture of life in the countryside is far from the truth. The farmer's life was in fact hard and insecure. The hillsides, with thin soil among bare rocks, could not support much agriculture, even with terracing. The only really fertile areas were in the plains. Modern research has shown that with carefully planned and intensive agriculture, Attica *could* have supported most or even all of the population. In practice, this did not happen, and Athens depended heavily on imported food.

The main crops were cereals (mainly barley, which needs less rain than wheat), vines and olives. The long roots of the olive tree make it especially suited to the hot, dry Mediterranean summer. The production of these crops meant hard work for the farmer, particularly at the May grain harvest, in September when the grapes were picked, and in October and November with the ploughing, sowing and olive harvest.

Ploughing and sowing

9

Farmers aimed to be self-sufficient in basic foods. Most holdings consisted of a number of small, scattered plots, with a wide variety of crops to spread the risk of starvation if one crop failed. A typical farm may have looked like this:

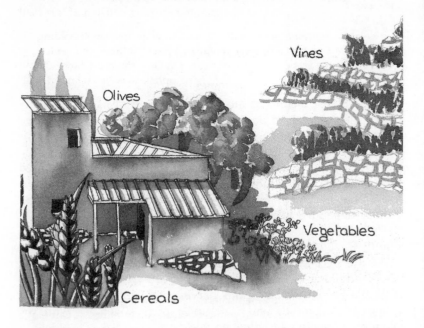

There was little low-lying land suitable for grazing, and few cattle. Sheep and goats provided cheese, milk and wool. Most of them were sent into the mountains in summer. This system is called *transhumance*. On the farm, oxen did the heavy work, as they still do in parts of Greece today. Horses were only kept by the rich for racing and for religious processions.

Food in the country was simple – bread and vegetables, with the occasional hare or bird. Festivals brought relaxation and a rare meat meal. Existence was precarious; bad weather or the farmer's absence at war (which was only too likely to coincide with the grain harvest, for the campaign season was spring and summer) were always in the country people's minds:

> We will pray to the gods
> to grant the Greeks wealth,
> that we may all harvest
> barley in plenty and plenty of wine
>   and figs to devour,
> that our wives may give birth,

that we may gather again
the blessings we've lost
and that red war may end.
[Aristophanes, *Peace* 1320–8]

Natural resources

The wealth of Attica lay in its mineral resources. Xenophon refers to

the unlimited quantities of stone which occur naturally, from which are built the finest temples and altars ... and thanks to the gods we have inexhaustible mines of silver; the silver-mining area is continually being extended. [Xenophon, *Ways and Means* 1.4–5]

The white marble for the Parthenon was brought by ox-cart from the quarries of Mount Pentelikon. Mount Hymettos also provided a good quality marble of a rather bluish colour. Limestone was plentiful.

The 'inexhaustible mines of silver' were at Laureion. They were the basis of Athens' power in the fifth century.

Themistocles was the only man who had the courage to come before the people and propose that the revenue from the silver mines at Laureion, which the Athenians had been in the habit of dividing among themselves, should be set aside and the money used to build triremes [warships] for the war. [Plutarch, *Themistocles* 4]

At this time (484–3 BC) the annual profits of the mines amounted to 100 talents: 600 000 times the average daily wage. With the war-ships built with this money, the Athenians shortly afterwards defeated the Persian fleet in the sea battle at Salamis.

Alcibiades recognised the fundamental importance of the silver mines when he was urging the Spartans to establish a permanent fort in Attica during the Peloponnesian War:

Athens will immediately be deprived of her revenues from the silver mines at Laureion. [Thucydides 6.91.7]

The existence of the mines changed village life in the region completely. Numbers of citizens were attracted there to take up leases on concessions. The foundations of strong towers have been found, no doubt for defence against the wretched slave workforce, who may have numbered as many as 40 000.

Lead was also mined at Laureion, but the Athenians were unaware of the iron deposits there. They imported all their iron.

Another rich resource for Athens was the iron-bearing clay. It was easy to work, and when fired turned the warm orange-red colour which is familiar from the many pots which survive today.

A certain amount of timber was brought from the hills of Attica; the rest was imported and used for ship-building and furniture.

2

City and citizens

In 480 BC the Persian army invaded Attica and set fire to the city of Athens. Almost all the buildings were damaged. But shortly afterwards a combined Greek fleet defeated the Persians in a great sea-battle at Salamis off Athens.

The Athenians learnt two lessons which they never forgot. The first was the need for strong defensive walls to protect the city; the second was that their real strength lay in their navy. When they returned to the city, their leading general, Themistocles, gave instructions that:

the whole population, men, women and children, should take part in the wall-building, sparing neither private nor public building that would in any way help the work, but demolishing all of them.   [Thucydides 1.90.3]

The wall could be entered through twelve gates. Twenty years later, the Athenians built two 'Long Walls' to link the city with the port, the Peiraieus, six kilometres away, and safeguard supplies by sea.

The most striking feature of Athens, which lies in a plain, is the Acropolis. This is a limestone rock 120 metres high, with steep sides, in the centre of the city. The word 'acropolis' means 'height of the city', and an acropolis was a common feature of Greek cities, which were built round hills of this sort for defence. The acropolis in Athens was the centre of the worship of Athene, the patron goddess of the city. In the second half of the fifth century, many new buildings were constructed there. They will be described later in this chapter.

To the north-west of the Acropolis lay the Areopagus or Crag of Ares (the god of war). From ancient times, this was the meeting place of the aristocratic Areopagus Council which had once ruled Athens. By the fifth century, the Council had lost much of its power and some of its prestige, and in 462 BC it was deprived of its last real power – its responsibility for the laws and the actions of officials.

If the hill of the Areopagus was the home of the old form of government, the Pnyx Hill was that of the new. Here, in the open air, the citizens of Athens met to discuss political and religious issues and to pass laws in the assembly (*ecclesia*).

Citizens

The citizens were not simply the whole population of Attica, and consequently the idea of being a citizen meant much more to the Athenians than it does to most people today.

'Our city is open to the world.'   [Pericles in Thucydides 2.39]

A view of the Acropolis and the theatre of Dionysos

The city of Athens may have been open: citizenship was certainly not. There were probably never more than 50000 citizens at any one time, and they guarded their rights and privileges jealously. It was very rare for outsiders to be admitted into this exclusive society within a society.

Qualifications

To qualify as a citizen, an Athenian had to fulfil three conditions:
1. He must be male;
2. he must have registered with his deme (local organisation) at the age of 18;
3. both his parents must be Athenians.

Before 451 BC, it had only been necessary for the father to be Athenian. Pericles proposed a law changing this. We cannot be sure why. Perhaps there was a flood of immigrants. Maybe the citizens were afraid that they would have difficulty marrying their daughters to citizens. But from this time the citizen body was effectively closed.

Duties and privileges

All citizens shared the same duties and privileges:
1. they were free from direct taxation;
2. they had the right to own land;
3. they were protected by the law, and could bring prosecutions and serve on juries;
4. they had full political rights.

Even though in practice the same people (known as *rhetores*, orators or politicians) probably made the speeches every time, the decision-making lay in the hands of the whole assembly.

This city is free, not ruled by one man. The people have sovereign power as year by year new men take office. The rich have no advantage and the poor have equal rights. [Euripides, *Suppliants* 405–7]

The agora

The agora, the main central area and market place of Athens, was also very important in the political life of the citizens. The word 'agora' is connected with Greek words meaning 'to sell' and 'to address a public meeting'.

The Council of 500 ('boulê')

One of the most important buildings in the agora was the *bouleuterion* or Council House, where the Council met. All meetings were open to the public.

The citizens were divided into ten tribes for political purposes, and each tribe chose fifty men by lot annually to serve in the *boulê*. (They regarded lot as a more democratic method of appointment than election.) Members of the *boulê* had to be citizens over the age of thirty, but otherwise no qualifications were needed; all citizens were thought capable.

The main job of the *boulê* was to prepare the agenda for the assembly, though it could be amended when it got there, and to see that the decisions of the assembly were carried out through the various committees and officials. The councillors did not themselves take decisions.

The Executive Committee ('prytaneis')

Each month the fifty councillors from one tribe were appointed by lot to serve as the *prytaneis* (members of the executive committee).

A model of part of the agora. The 'tholos' is in the foreground

At the beginning of the fifth century they had their own building (the Prytaneum) just outside the agora, where a sacred fire was kept always alight as a symbol of the life of the city. Later they moved to a round building in the agora called the *tholos*. Here they worked, ate and slept for their 35–36 days of office.

Their chairman (*epistates*) was appointed daily, again by lot, and no-one could do the job twice. If an assembly was to be held that day, the *epistates* was its president.

The state officers

The agora also contained the offices of the most important officers of the city. These posts, like the *boulê*, were open to any citizen over the age of thirty. The Athenians, as we have seen, were determined to prevent individuals from acquiring too much power, and they checked their officials in various ways:
1. Offices were held in rotation and usually for one year only.
2. Most offices were filled by lot, not by election.
3. Most officials were grouped in boards of ten.
4. Every official had his qualifications and actions in office carefully scrutinised by the people.

The generals ('strategoi')

The most important officers of state were the ten generals who took charge of the army and navy and had overall command in war. The Athenians recognised the need for expertise and experience in this field, and the generals were elected rather than chosen by lot. They were also unlike other officials in that they could be re-elected year after year. Pericles, for example, was general fifteen times from 443 BC to his death in 429 BC.

The generals attended the assembly, where they were in theory at least on a level with any other citizen. No doubt their speeches were listened to with attention, but they could not influence decisions because of their office.

The headquarters of the generals was in the agora.

Other public buildings

The agora also contained the offices of the Polemarch, who dealt with the legal affairs of foreigners who lived in the city (see Chapter 3), and the Eponymous Archon, who gave his name to the year in which he held office. He dealt with some tax and inheritance cases. The King Archon, who organised festivals and dealt with blasphemy trials, had his office in the Royal Stoa (also known as the Stoa of Zeus). A stoa was a covered colonnade. There were three in the agora, decorated with paintings and statues, and people met, strolled and chatted in their shade.

The city mint was also in the agora, and the prison, which was used for debtors and people awaiting trial or execution; imprisonment was not a normal punishment in itself.

Ostracism

Once a year, if the assembly had voted for it, the central area of the agora was fenced off for an ostracism. This involved the citizens voting to send any individual into exile for ten years. This was another way of preventing too much power falling into the hands of any individuals, but some people tried to manipulate the system to get rid of their political opponents.

Citizens who wished to take part scratched the name of the person they wanted exiled on a piece of pottery and entered through the gates in the fenced-off area to cast their vote. If anyone's name appeared more than 6000 times, he was compelled to leave Athens, but his property was not confiscated. Many of these pieces of pottery (*ostraka*) have been found in the agora. A pot was discovered containing dozens with Themistocles' name on – all in the same handwriting. Either a professional writer was helping out the illiterate, or some cheating was going on!

Lawcourts

STUDENT: And this, you see, is the map of the whole world. Look, here's Athens.
OLD FARMER: Can't be; if it's Athens, where are the jurymen?

[Aristophanes, *Clouds* 207–8]

The Athenians were famous – or notorious – for their lawcourts. There were no judges, and the juries, which consisted of between 201 and 2501 men depending on the case, were judge and jury combined. There was a roll of 6000 volunteers to serve on juries annually. They were assigned to the different courts, the Heliaia and the *dikasteria*, by a complicated procedure on the morning of the trials. This system, and the size of the juries, were designed to prevent corruption.

There were no state prosecutions. Injured parties had to bring individual prosecutions against those who had wronged them. Anyone could bring a public prosecution (called a *graphe* or writ because it had to be in writing). To prevent irresponsible prosecutions, there were laws to punish unsuccessful prosecutors.

In his comedy *Wasps*, Aristophanes mocks the Athenians' enthusiasm for sitting on juries. He caricatures the jurymen as irritable old men, only interested in finding anyone and everyone guilty – and then picking up their pay, which was two obols a day, rising later to three, half the wage of a skilled workman. A slave is speaking here:

'I'll tell you what the old man's trouble really is. He's what they call a trialophile or litigious maniac – the worst case I've ever come across. What he's addicted to is serving on juries and he moans like anything if he can't get a front seat at every trial.' [Aristophanes, *Wasps* 87–90]

Nevertheless, the Athenians regarded their jury service as an important part of their democratic rights.

What is frequently said about public lawsuits is quite right; very often private quarrels correct public wrongs. [Aeschines 1.1–2]

The agora had other purposes besides political ones, however.

Entertainment

Until the middle of the century, competitions in drama were probably held in the agora. Wooden stands were erected for the spectators, but one of these collapsed during a performance. The Athenians then established a permanent theatre on the south slope of the Acropolis, near the temple of Dionysos, god of drama.

A concert hall called the Odeion was built to the east of the theatre:

Pericles had a decree passed to establish a musical festival. He himself was elected one of the stewards and laid down rules as to how the competitors should sing or play the pipe or the lyre. [Plutarch, *Pericles* 13.6]

Religion

The boundary of the agora was marked by stones, and the whole area was a religious precinct containing temples, statues and altars. There were temples to Zeus, the chief god; the Mother of the gods; Apollo, the god of music, archery, prophecy and medicine; and Hephaistos, the fire and smith god, who was worshipped mainly by craftsmen.

The commercial life of the agora will be described in Chapter 6.

Pericles' building programme

The busy life of the city centred on the agora. But the most famous religious buildings of Athens, and the greatest works of art and architecture, were on the Acropolis. Again, Pericles played a leading role:

Pericles boldly laid before the people proposals for immense public works and plans for buildings, which would involve many different arts and industries and require long periods to complete, his object being that those who stayed at home, no less than those serving in the fleet or army or on garrison duty, should be enabled to enjoy a share of the national wealth.   [Plutarch, *Pericles* 12.5]

Plutarch gives us an idea of the scale of the operation:

The materials to be used were stone, bronze, ivory, gold, ebony and cypress wood, while the arts or trades which wrought or fashioned them were those of carpenter, modeller, copper-smith, stone-mason, dyer, worker in gold and ivory, painter, embroiderer and engraver, and besides these the carriers and suppliers of the materials, such as merchants, sailors, and pilots for the sea-borne traffic, and waggon-makers, trainers of draught animals, and drivers for everything that came by land. There were also rope-makers, weavers, leather-workers, roadbuilders and miners.   [Plutarch, *Pericles* 12.6]

Today, you can still see the temple of Athene the Virgin (the Parthenon), the Propylaia or Gateway, the temple of Erechtheus and the temple of Athene Nike (Victory). But the statues, sculptures and paintings which added to the magnificence of the Acropolis site have largely disappeared, with the exception of the sculptures of the Parthenon, known as the Elgin Marbles, which are in the British Museum.

So the buildings arose, as imposing in their sheer size as they were inimitable in the grace of their outlines, since the artists strove to excel themselves in the beauty of their workmanship.   [Plutarch, *Pericles* 13.1]

The outstanding architects, sculptors and painters of the time worked on the buildings and statues:

The director and supervisor of the whole enterprise was Pheidias, although there were various great architects and artists employed on the individual buildings. For example, Kallikrates and Iktinos were the architects of the Parthenon . . .   [Plutarch, *Pericles* 13.4]

There was some criticism by Pericles' opponents at the time of his decision to spend the contributions of Athens' allies on the project:

> The Greeks must be outraged when they see that we are gilding and beautifying our city, as if it were some vain woman decking herself out with costly stones and statues and temples worth millions of money.
>
> [Plutarch, *Pericles* 12.2]

But future generations have agreed with Plutarch's judgement at the end of the first century AD:

> A bloom of eternal freshness hovers over these works of his and preserves them from the touch of time, as if some unfading spirit of youth, some ageless vitality had been breathed into them.　　[Plutarch, *Pericles* 13.3]

This was the environment in which the Athenians lived, the city for which they were prepared to fight.

Military service

Athens was almost always at war during the fifth century and permanently so from 431 to 404 BC. The poorest citizens (called 'thetes') rowed in the fleet. They became increasingly important and confident as Athens came to rely more and more on the triremes. Pericles pointed out how powerful the city was:

> With your navy as it is today there is no power under the sun which can stop you sailing where you wish. This power of yours is something in an altogether different category from all the advantages of houses or cultivated land.　　[Thucydides 2.62]

Better-off citizens served in the army as hoplites. These were infantry soldiers armed with a heavy round shield, a sword, a spear, a helmet, a breastplate and leg-guards (greaves). Each man had to provide his own equipment, but the sons of men who died in battle were provided with armour by the state.

The hoplites fought in a close formation called a phalanx, where each man depended on the man next to him. This method of fighting must have increased the bond among the citizens.

Loss of citizen rights

It is easy to see why an Athenian citizen feared to lose his rights. *Atimia* or loss of rights might be inflicted as a legal punishment in a more severe form which involved confiscation of property and exile or a less severe one which did not. But in either case *atimia* meant shame and very tangible disadvantages.

The citizen might lose his rights to:
1. hold any political or religious office;
2. be a herald or an ambassador;
3. speak in the *ecclesia* or serve on the *Boulê*;
4. enter the agora;
5. visit the sanctuaries or take part in sacrifices;
6. go to law, serve on a jury or be a witness;
7. serve in the army.

Atimia in its extreme form made a man a virtual outlaw, unable to carry out any of the activities which gave him his identity – and superiority – as a citizen.

Home life

Not even the Athenian male could spend quite all of his time in public, engaged on the affairs of his city. The last part of this chapter looks at the citizens' lives at home.

Hoplites going to war

The citizen and his household

Every citizen was the *kyrios* (governor or lord) of his household. According to Aristotle, he governed his slaves as a master, his children as a king and his wife as a political leader.

As only citizens could own land, the maintenance of his *kleros*, or family property, was one of a citizen's chief duties. His aim was to pass it intact to a successor within the family. Women could not inherit – they were perpetual minors and had to have a *kyrios* all their lives. A man who had no sons might adopt one to get an heir. If he died leaving only a daughter, she was known as an *epikleros*. She was at once married off to the nearest male relative.

The *kyrios* was responsible for the family worship. He was also expected to join in the festivals of his *phratria*, or family organisation, and take an interest in local affairs.

Private houses

In our own homes we find a beauty and good taste which delight us and drive away our cares.   [Thucydides 2.38]

In fact, the Athenians paid far more attention to their public buildings than to their homes. This was partly because the men did not spend much time at home, partly as a matter of principle. A

Athenian houses

23

century later, the orator Demosthenes noted with disapproval how things had changed:

The buildings which our ancestors left to adorn the city – the temples and harbours and all that goes with them – are on a scale which their successors cannot hope to surpass. Look at the Propylaia, the docks, the stoas . . . And the private houses of those in power then were modest and in keeping with our democratic ideas of equality.
[Demosthenes, *On Organisation* 13.28–9]

According to Demosthenes, some individuals in his day built houses even grander than the public buildings.

Even in the fifth century not all houses were the same size. Most were not large, however, even if they had a second storey:

In the first place I must explain that I have a small house on two floors, of equal size upstairs and downstairs, that is in the women's and men's quarters. [Lysias, 1.9]

Limestone and marble were used for the temples and public buildings: houses were made of unbaked clay bricks on foundations of small stones and clay. All that could be seen from the street, unless the front part of the house was let out as a shop, was a long wall with one or two high windows and a single door. The women who lived inside were effectively shut off from the world.

Through the doorway, a passage usually led to a courtyard, with an altar to Zeus Herkeios (God of Boundaries) and sometimes a well. If there was no well, slaves would fetch water from the fountains in the streets.

As we have seen, men and women had their own quarters. The *andron* or 'room for men' was regarded as the most important room in the house. It was the only one likely to have a mosaic floor and painted walls. Other floors were simply beaten earth. Even this room had little furniture. Couches covered with rugs and blankets doubled as beds. There were small tables and chairs with curved backs. A type of dresser might hold statues and drinking vessels. There were hooks on the walls.

Since both indoor and outdoor tasks require work and attention, the gods prepare the soul of the woman for the indoor work and concerns and the soul of the man for the outdoor work. [Xenophon, *Oeconomicus* 7.22–3]

This convenient arrangement meant that the men did the shopping in the agora, while the women took responsibility for the organisation of the house. Girls received some basic training from their mothers:

When she came to me, she just knew how to produce a cloak from the wool given to her and see the spinning given to the maids.

[Xenophon, Oeconomicus 7.5–6]

Ischomachos, an upper-class Athenian, is here talking to Socrates about his young wife.

Not only did the wife have the difficult and time-consuming job of spinning and weaving wool for all the clothes and rugs for the household, but she also had to supervise the slaves, look after any who were ill, ensure that there were adequate food supplies and grind grain for bread. A well-ordered house was a source of pride:

How good it is to keep one's stock of utensils in order, and how easy to find a suitable place in the house to keep each set in! What a beautiful sight is afforded by boots of all sorts arranged in rows! How beautiful it is to see cloaks of all sorts kept separate, or blankets or bronze vessels or table furniture! [Xenophon, *Oeconomicus* 8.19]

3

Metics and slaves

Foreigners who chose to live permanently in Athens were known as metics (*metoikoi*).

Thousands of non-Athenians came to see the city which Pericles declared 'an education to Greece'. They came to sight-see, to watch the plays and join in the religious processions. Many chose to stay. The majority were attracted by the advantages of living in a powerful and prosperous city and by the opportunities for making a living. Some few were refugees from their own states or had friends in Athens. Not surprisingly, many settled in the Peiraieus and joined in the busy commercial life there.

Work

Most metics became craftsmen and traders. They did ordinary jobs and most probably remained poor all their lives. When the Erechtheion temple was being built on the Acropolis, we know from the accounts that twenty metics worked alongside slaves and citizens for the same wage – a drachma a day.

From a list made in 401 BC we know that metics were farmers, bakers, statuette-makers, mule-drivers, gardeners, carpenters, oil-merchants, bath-makers, fullers and nut-sellers.

A few metics became rich. Cephalos came from Syracuse to Athens, partly because he was a friend of Pericles. His son Lysias was a speech-writer and had been 'the richest of the metics' until his property was sold off in 404 BC for no less than 70 talents. This included his shield factory.

Status

Some metics mixed socially with citizens. The philosopher Socrates and his upper-class friends met in the house where Cephalos lived in the Peiraieus, for example. But there was a fundamental difference in status between even the richest metic and the poorest citizen.

Metics were debarred from owning property in Attica. The farmer mentioned on the 401 BC list was employed on someone else's land. Even the richest metics had to have a citizen landlord.

Metics were also prevented from having any part in politics. They could not attend the *ecclesia* or take any part in decisions which might affect their lives. They had to be represented by an Athenian patron (*prostates*) and pay a special metic's tax of a drachma a month. They were also expected to finance warships and choruses if they were rich, and to serve in the army regularly and the navy in cases of emergency.

Religion

Metics brought their own religion and were allowed complete freedom of worship. In fact, the Athenian citizens were happy to take part in the worship of the eastern goddesses, Bendis and Cybele. The torch-race on horseback during Bendis' festival attracted especial interest.

A helmet-maker at work

Metics also participated in the worship of the Athenian gods. They watched the plays at the festival of Dionysos and had a special part to play in the great procession of the Panathenaia.

In spite of the many disadvantages of metic status, foreigners continued to be eager to settle in Athens. When the Peloponnesian War broke out in 431 BC, there were at least 3000 metics in the Athenian army. One calculation suggests that there were about 10000 male metics, as well as their wives and children – a substantial proportion of the population.

Slaves

Those who can do so buy slaves to share their work with them.
[Xenophon, *Memorabilia* 2.3.3]

The Greeks considered it normal and right to keep non-Greeks as slaves.

It is thought wrong to enslave friends, but right to enslave enemies. [Xenophon, *Memorabilia* 2.2.2]

In private life we regard it as right to use barbarians as slaves.
[Isocrates 4.181]

This idea was questioned by a few individuals at the end of the fifth century, but in the fourth century the philosopher Aristotle answered them with his theory of 'natural slavery':

Well, it is clear that there are some who are naturally free or naturally slaves. For them, slavery is both a necessary system and a moral one. [Aristotle, *Politics* I.5]

Slaves were on the very margins of human society, classed among 'living tools'.

Sources of slaves

Prisoners captured in war were regularly enslaved – after all, they owed their very lives to their captors. There was also a regular peacetime slave trade which centred on the island of Delos in the Aegean Sea.

Asia and the Black Sea coast were common sources of slaves. When the property of a man called Cephisodoros, who lived in the Peiraieus, was sold in 414 BC, it included three female and two male slaves from Thrace, a male from Syria, a male from Illyria, and a male, a boy and a 'little boy' from Caria.

Some slaves were born into slavery, like this high-minded man in a play by Euripides:

Born to service as I am, I would like to be numbered among the noble slaves, unfree in name, free in mind.   [Euripides, *Helen* 728–31]

Work

Less wealthy families probably had more female than male slaves. The Trojan queen Hecabe imagines a slave's life in terms which would have been familiar in Athens:

And finally, to cap all my miseries, I shall have to go to Greece in my old age as a slave woman: they will load me with tasks most unsuitable for my age – keeping the door, guarding the keys, making the bread.

[Euripides, *Trojan Women* 489–911]

Women did the work inside the house. The orator Demosthenes tells how an intruder into a house found the male slaves working on the land outside, and the females shut up making clothes.

Apart from domestic work, female slaves provided all forms of entertainment. Nicarete, an enterprising Corinthian woman, brought up seven girls to be prostitutes, and made a tidy profit when all seven persuaded their lovers to buy their freedom. No doubt the same happened in Athens; Aspasia, Pericles' foreign mistress, was rumoured to run a brothel. Paintings and literature show that female slaves danced and played music at parties. Their price was controlled by the town officials.

Male slaves worked alongside free men in most forms of work – crafts, trade and even mining, though there the workforce was largely made up of slaves:

Nicias once owned 1000 slaves in the silver mines, and he hired them out to Sosias the Thracian on condition that Sosias paid one obol per day per slave, and always kept the same number.   [Xenophon, *Revenues* 4.14]

Given the condition in the mines, the last statement is understandable.

It was quite common for slaves to be hired out, or for them to find their own employment and pay a fixed amount of their earnings to their masters. The orator Aeschines refers to a man who owned nine or ten skilled cobblers who paid him two obols of their earnings a day.

Some slaves were owned not by individuals, but by the city. The 'police force' in Athens consisted of slaves called Scythian Archers. Their status was high in comparison with other slaves, but they could not arrest or prosecute anyone. State-owned slaves also worked as road-menders, as the executioner, in public records and in the mint.

Value of slaves

Slaves were not essential to the economy of Athens, but they were valuable property in that they could be sold and in that they produced wealth. Xenophon calculated that the state might own up to 10000 slaves, and that this number would bring in an annual revenue of 100 talents. Demosthenes' father 'received an annual revenue of not less than 30 minai clear profit' from the 33 slaves working in his sword factory.

Most valuable of all, slaves released the wealthier citizens of Athens to spend their time in a way befitting a gentleman – politics and conversation with friends.

The price of slaves depended on their looks, strength and skills. Sometimes a master would buy slaves unskilled and train them himself; others preferred to buy them already trained. In this case they might command high prices:

Nicias is said to have paid a talent for a manager of his silver mines. [Xenophon, *Memorabilia* 2.5.2]

Treatment

Socrates, according to Xenophon, lists slaves with houses, land, farm animals and equipment as being 'things that are both acquired and looked after with care' (*Memorabilia* 2.4.2).

A slave was regarded as a full member of the household, for he or she shared the house and its food supply. In the fourth century, a new slave entering the house was showered with fruit and nuts by the mistress, as she had been herself when she entered as a bride. It is likely that this was an old custom.

Slaves were introduced into the worship of the family gods and took part in religious festivals. Care of sick slaves was an important part of a wife's duties.

In the streets, it was impossible to tell the difference between slaves and free men – much to the disgust of the traditionally minded.

Now as for the slaves and foreigners who live in Athens, they lead a most undisciplined life: you are not permitted to hit them, and a slave will not stand out of the way for you ... The Athenians allow their slaves to live in the lap of luxury, and some of them indeed live a life of real magnificence ... In the matter of free speech, we put slaves on equal terms with free men.   [Old Oligarch I, 10–11]

This picture is undoubtedly exaggerated, but there is evidence that the Athenians treated their slaves quite well. The cheeky slave who outwits his master is such a common character in Aristophanes' comedies that it is hard to believe that he is utterly unrealistic. The Athenians also trusted their slaves with some important tasks, such as escorting their children to school and supervising them there. Some teachers were also slaves.

However, the Athenians were not generous in giving slaves their freedom. Some few examples are known, like the prostitutes bought out of slavery by their lovers. Demosthenes' father freed a slave called Miyas in his will. The case of Pasion the banker in the fourth century was extremely rare: he gained not only his freedom but citizenship as well and died very rich indeed. Normally a freed slave was given the status of a metic.

The picture has another side. Slaves could run away and take refuge at the shrine of Theseus, but they were not released from

A slave in a comedy carrying a calf

their master unless they could persuade someone else to buy them. When the Spartans set up a permanent fort on the borders of Attica in 413 BC, Thucydides says that 20 000 slaves, mostly craftsmen, ran away from their owners and joined the Spartans.

Slaves were usually uprooted forcibly from their homes and taken to a foreign land where they were completely dependent on their owners. They would never see their families again. They had no rights in Athenian law, they could not own possessions or contract legal relationships and they were tortured to extract evidence for court cases because they were regarded as untrustworthy.

Slaves, freedmen and foreigners faced hostility and prejudice:

I am ashamed to speak of Hyperbolos – his father is even now a branded slave in the public silver mint, and he himself, non-Greek foreigner that he is, makes lamps. [Andocides, frg. 5]

A few masters bred children from slaves and regarded this as a way of making sure they behaved well, but Socrates asked his friend Aristippos:

'Do masters not cure their slaves' sexual desires by starvation, prevent them from stealing by keeping their goods locked up, put them in chains and flog them for idleness?'

Aristippos replied:

'I use every kind of punishment to reduce them to submission.'
[Xenophon, *Memorabilia* 2.1.16–17]

Plato in the fourth century sums up a general attitude:

There is nothing healthy in the soul of a slave. A sensible man should not entrust them with anything. [Plato, *Laws* 776b–8a]

4

Religion

The place of religion

For many people today, religion is only important on life's great occasions – birth, marriage and death. There is a wide variety of belief in multi-cultural societies like modern England.

Religion was very different for the Athenians: it was a vital part of their everyday lives. The gods literally came first in everything – meetings of the assembly started with the sacrifice of a pig and religious rites; anyone undertaking any risky enterprise would attempt to find out the will of the gods first; speeches, parties and letters started with prayers and promises.

I assume that it is right for anyone who is embarking on any serious discussion and task to begin first with the gods. [Demosthenes, Letter 1.1]

At home, the *kyrios* was in charge of family prayers and offerings. Outside, the Athenians – men *and* women, for religion was a sphere where the women were important – watched and took part in numerous ceremonies. There were statues, altars, sanctuaries and temples in the city and the countryside to remind them of the gods.

There is plenty of evidence for the Athenians' rituals and religious practices. It is less easy to uncover the beliefs that lay behind them. There was no holy book like the Qur'an or the Bible. However, most people seem to have held the same views about the gods – who they were, how they should be worshipped, how they intervened in human affairs – and had much the same hopes and fears about them.

This is not to say that the Athenians did not discuss or question their beliefs. We shall consider the views of some of the critics of religion at the end of this chapter. But very few people saw any reason to change the religious practices which they believed had brought them success in the past:

By performing the proper sacrifices, our ancestors left our city the most powerful and prosperous in Greece. It is therefore right that we offer the same sacrifices as they did, if only for the sake of the good fortune which has resulted. [Lysias, 30.18]

The gods

The Athenians believed in many gods. The most important were the Olympians, a family of twelve gods and goddesses believed to live on Mount Olympus in northern Greece. Zeus, 'father of gods and men', was at their head, but he was not thought to have created the universe or even to have existed at its beginning. Ancient gods like Chaos and Night had existed long before him.

Below the earth lay the underworld, ruled over by Zeus' brother, Hades. There were many other terrifying powers below the earth, such as the avenging Erinyes or Furies, who pursued the wicked in life and death.

In the countryside, other deities demanded respect, among them the goat-god, Pan, who made flocks fertile, and the nymphs, female spirits of mountains, streams and woods. Also important were the cults of local heroes, such as Theseus, the legendary founder of Athens.

The gods had human forms and their own spheres of influence. They were not thought to enter into loving relationships with humans (though Greek mythology is full of stories of gods' sexual relations with mortal women).

It would be odd for anybody to make out that he loved Zeus.
[Aristotle, MM 1208b 30]

The gods did not impose a code of moral behaviour which they demanded humans should follow. But they did demand recognition of their power, and they would respond to due sacrifice and prayer. Priests and priestesses were therefore appointed to ensure that the correct rituals were carried out.

Wise men offer prayers for their fruit and crops and cattle and horses and sheep, in fact, for all that they possess. [Xenophon, *Oeconomicus* 5.20]

Gods and goddesses

The seven gods and goddesses mentioned here seem to have been regarded by the Athenians as the most important. More festival days were devoted to them than to the other gods.

Athene

City and land generally are sacred to Athene. No matter how the worship of other gods is established in the villages, they hold Athene in just as much honour. [Pausanias 1.26.6]

> Pallas Athene, our city's protector,
> queen of a land
> supreme in piety,
> mighty in war,
> rich in poets,
> come to us.
>
> [Aristophanes, *Knights* 581–6]

The city of Athens was named after Athene. Every Athenian child learned of her contest with Poseidon, the sea god, for the land of Attica. He gave the gift of water, but she offered the more valuable olive tree. This was the subject of the sculptures at the west end of her main temple, the Parthenon. Athene was the chief – though not the only – goddess worshipped on the Acropolis, and her temples there dominated the city. Every year there was an all-Athenian festival in her honour.

Demeter and Dionysos

The pattern of worship in Athens was related to the agricultural year. Two gods closely associated with farming and the country-side had even more festival days devoted to them than did Athene.

Demeter, worshipped with her daughter Persephone (or simply Kore, the girl), was goddess of corn and fertility. Her worship, which centred on Eleusis, fourteen miles from Athens, is described later in this chapter.

Dionysos was god of wine and crops. He represented a wilder, more emotional side to Greek religion.

The proper worship of these two was vital to ensure the success of sowing and harvesting.

Zeus

Zeus was important to the Athenians not only as the chief god and father of Athene, but also as god of the home and property. Most houses had an altar to Zeus Herkeios (God of Boundaries) in the courtyard. He was believed to protect the house from intruders.

Athene

Hermes

Outside private houses and public buildings, and along tracks in the country, stood statues of Hermes, god of travellers, merchants and flocks. One night in 415 BC, most of these Herms, as they were called, were badly damaged. There was a genuine and universal sense of outrage.

Artemis and Apollo

Artemis, the huntress and goddess of wild creatures and places, was worshipped at Brauron. Little girls danced in her honour in saffron-coloured dresses, perhaps to imitate the hide of a bear, an animal particularly associated with the goddess.

Artemis' twin brother, Apollo, was god of music, archery, prophecy, medicine and the care of flocks and herds.

Divination

Divination is the name given to human attempts to discover the will of the gods. The gods might cooperate:

The gods know everything and they give forewarnings to anyone they choose through sacrifices, omens, voices, and dreams.

[Xenophon, *Eq. Mag.* 9, 7–9]

The insides of sacrificed animals, especially the liver, were examined to discover signs of the future. Omens were sent by the gods in various ways. Some people would spend the night in a temple or shrine in the hope of receiving the advice of the gods. Both private citizens and the state regularly consulted Apollo at his shrine at Delphi. Here the famous and highly respected oracle was consulted on very specific questions, often concerned with religion or war. The questioner usually posed the question in the form: 'Is it more agreeable and better to...?' The priestess, supposedly possessed by the god, gave an answer which was interpreted by the priests.

The flight and behaviour of birds was another recognised method of telling the will of the gods:

As I sat on the ancient seat of augury,
in the sanctuary where every bird I know
will hover at my hands – suddenly I heard it,
a strange voice in the wingbeats, unintelligible,
barbaric, a mad scream! Talons flashing, ripping,

they were killing each other – that much I knew –
the murderous fury whirring in those wings
made that much clear!

[Sophocles, *Antigone* 999–1004]

The prophet Teiresias, who is speaking here, warns the king that this unusual behaviour on the part of the birds means that he has committed a great sin and death will follow.

Any unusual occurrence, such as a weasel crossing the road, called for interpretation and avoiding action – at least by the superstitious. Theophrastus, a philosopher who lived in the fourth and third centuries BC, made fun of such people:

He washes his hands and sprinkles himself with water from the Three Springs and before he goes out for the day he puts a laurel-leaf from nearby a temple in his mouth. If a cat runs across the road, he refuses to move until someone else has passed or he has thrown three pebbles across the road. [Theophrastus, *Characters* 16]

Dreams were a common indication of the future, but they could be deceptive:

Now to Zeus' mind this thing appeared to be the best counsel, to send evil Dream to Atreus' son Agamemnon. [Homer, *Iliad* 2, 5–6]

The difficulty of interpreting such signs from the gods led many people to consult professional soothsayers or *manteis*, and this is still something of a passion among Mediterranean peoples. But the Athenians usually felt confident in their own abilities and acted on their own without the help of divination. Nicias was an exception:

Nicias was one of those deeply in awe of the supernatural and he relied heavily on divination. He sacrificed daily to the gods and kept a *mantis* at his house, supposedly for consultations about state business, but in fact mostly for his private affairs. [Plutarch, *Nicias* 4. 1–2]

Most Athenians regarded Nicias' superstition as a joke. Aristophanes made fun of it in his play *Amphiaraos*, produced in 414 BC. But when this characteristic influenced Nicias' military judgement, disaster followed for the Athenian expedition to Sicily. Thucydides makes his disapproval clear:

When everything was ready and they were just about to sail, there was an eclipse of the moon ... Most of the Athenians were alarmed by this and urged the generals to wait, and Nicias, who was rather over-inclined to divination and that kind of thing, said that he was not prepared even to discuss the move until they had waited the thrice nine days recommended by the *manteis*. [Thucydides, 7.50.4]

Prayer

The Athenians prayed standing up, with their hands raised. Prayers were simple in form; the worshipper called on the god, stated his or her claim in terms of previous services rendered to or by the god, promised recompense for future favours and ended with the request. Here is a typical prayer:

First I call upon you, daughter of Zeus, immortal Athene, and Artemis, guardian of the city, the fair-famed one sitting on your throne in the agora, and brother Apollo who shoots from afar, o three saviours, appear to me. If ever before you have turned aside the fire of evil and averted the destruction rushing on the city, come now also.

[Sophocles, *Oedipus the King* 158–66]

Sacrifice

When they had dined, as you would expect, since one was sacrificing to Zeus Ktesios and entertaining his friend, and the other was about to sail and being entertained to dinner, they made libations and put frankincense on the altar for their own safety and prosperity.　　　[Antiphon 1.18]

Sacrifices might consist of an offering of grain, fruit, cakes or incense on an altar, or a drink-offering or libation of wine, milk or oil poured on the ground. The god's help was expected as a result.

The sacrifice of an animal was considered most valuable. Bulls,

A sacrifice in front of a Herm

cows, sheep or goats were the most common. They should have no faults in them. They were decorated with garlands of flowers or gilt on their horns and (it was hoped) walked willingly to the altar. The crowd remained silent to avoid speaking words of bad luck. A basket containing barley grains and the sacrificial knife was carried round the altar. The priest took a burning stick from the fire on the altar, dipped it in pure water and sprinkled it over the sacrificial victim and the people. He then washed his hands, made a first offering of barley grains and cut off a little of the victim's hair to throw on the fire. Prayers were spoken. While the victim was stunned and its throat cut, a flute was played and the women cried aloud. The blood was caught in a bowl.

In one type of sacrifice (a holocaust), the entire victim was burnt; more commonly, the carcase was skinned and cut up. Part was burnt on the altar for the god, the rest cooked and distributed among the grateful population.

Festivals

'When our work is over, we are in a position to enjoy all kinds of recreation for our spirits. There are various kinds of contests and sacrifices regularly throughout the year.'   [Pericles, in Thucydides 2.38]

In a society without weekends, relaxation was one important aspect of religious festivals. All of them had common elements: purification, sacrifices, processions and contests. But the main festivals had individual characters. The chart which follows gives some of the festivals of the Athenian year. Two of them – the Great Panathenaia and the Eleusinian mysteries – are then described in more detail.

Month	Festival	Events
Hecatombaion (June–July)	Kronia	In honour of Zeus' father, Kronos. Masters and slaves feasted together
	Panathenaia	See pages 43–4
Boedromion (August–September)	Greater Mysteries of Eleusis	See pages 44–6
Pyanepsion (September–October)	Oskophoria	Procession. Two noble young men carried branches laden with grapes

Month	Festival	Events
	Pyanepsia	In honour of Apollo. Olive branches wreathed with wool and hung with figs, loaves and pots of honey, oil and wine were hung outside the houses
	Thesmophoria	3-day fertility festival for women only, in honour of Demeter: (1) procession to Eleusis; (2) fast; (3) sacrifices: putrefied remains of piglets mixed with corn seed on altar
	Apatouria	Phratria (clan) festival at local cult centres. Communal meal, sacrifice, admission of new members. See page 51
Posideion (November–December)	Haloa	Fertility festival for men and women in honour of Dionysos and Demeter at Eleusis. No blood sacrifices
	Rural Dionysia	Procession with phallos to make the corn grow. Procession and performance of comedies in honour of Dionysos
Gamelion (December–January)	Lenaia	Procession and performance of comedies in the theatre of Dionysos
Anthesterion (January–February)	Anthesteria	3-day flower festival in honour of Dionysos: (1) Jars – wine of new vintage tasted; (2) Jugs – offerings to Dionysos and drinking contest; (3) Pots – polluted day devoted to the dead. See pages 51 and 61

Month	Festival	Events
	Lesser Eleusinian Mysteries of Kore (Demeter's daughter Persephone)	Celebrated at Agrai. Sacrifice of sow, procession with myrtle branches and seeds and grain. Preparation for Greater Mysteries – oath of secrecy by worshippers
Elaphebolion (February–March)	Great or City Dionysia	Celebration of the arrival of Dionysos. Procession with *phalloi*. Sacrifices. Competitions in choral singing, tragedies and comedies. See page 79
Thargelion (April–May)	Thargelia	Harvest festival in honour of Apollo and Artemis. Boys carried branches wreathed with wool and first fruits. *Thargelos* means vegetables boiled in a pot. Two ugly men beaten through the streets as scapegoats
	Kallynteria	Sweeping of the temple of Athene
	Plynteria	The statue of Athene was taken out and bathed in the sea. No work allowed, sanctuaries roped off. A dangerous and unlucky day
	Theseia	In honour of Theseus, the legendary founder of Athens. Poor people were given bread and meat
Skirophorion (May–June)	Skira	Women only. Offerings to Athene, Poseidon and Demeter. Piglets thrown into pits for the Thesmophoria
	Arrephoria	Two noble girls at night carried on their heads

See page 79

Month	Festival	Events
		unknown sacred objects given them by Athene's priestess. They left them in the Garden of Aphrodite at the foot of the Acropolis and brought something else back

The Panathenaic Festivals

Two Panathenaic festivals are held at Athens, one annually and one, called the Great Panathenaia, every four years.   [Harpocration, *Lexicon*]

The Athenians believed that this festival was their oldest as well as the most important:

The feast and competition of the Panathenaia was originally established by Erichthonius, son of Hephaistos and Athene, and reinstituted by Theseus.   [Scholiast to Plato, *Parmenides* 127a]

The Great Panathenaia was celebrated just after the first new moon of the year, on 28 Hekatombaion. This day was believed to be Athene's birthday, on which she sprang fully grown and dressed in armour, from the head of Zeus. The arrangements for the festival were so complicated that a board of ten officials, called *Athlothetai*, were appointed for a four-year term. For the last hectic 24 days, they were fed at the public expense.

The festival began with all-night singing and dancing on the Acropolis (called a *pannychis*), a dawn procession, a sacrifice and a feast. By the late fifth century, there were contests in dithyramb (choral songs to Dionysos) and dancing. Athletic contests and horse races were also held.

The prizes were sets of 'Panathenaic amphorai', pots two foot high filled with sacred oil. On the front was a black-figure Athene with a spear; on the back a picture of the appropriate contest.

There were also contests between musicians and rhapsodes, who recited the poems of Homer. Some contests were limited to citizens, like the 'contest in manliness' in which teams from the tribes competed in size and strength.

There was also a torch race, where each competitor had to run from an altar in the Academy gymnasium to the altar of Athene on the Acropolis without his torch going out. The boat race off Cape Sounion was between triremes provided and manned by each tribe.

The climax of the festival was a great procession to escort a new robe (*peplos*) for Athene Polias, Protector of the City, to her ancient olive-wood statue, the most holy object on the Acropolis. The new *peplos* was woven over a period of nine months by girls from noble families. The procession is illustrated on the frieze of the Parthenon. It included the girls who had made the *peplos*, girls carrying baskets of grain for the sacrifice on their heads, metics wearing purple robes and carrying trays of offerings, old men with olive branches, allies and colonists bringing cows for sacrifice and weapons, as required by law. There were also hoplites, chariots, cavalry, marshals and the Athenian officials.

After the *peplos* had been presented, there was a great sacrifice of cows and sheep, and everyone had a chance to eat and drink. The festival gave the Athenians a powerful sense of the magnificence and power of their city under the protection of Athene.

The Eleusinian Mysteries

When Demeter came to our land . . . her gracious favour to our ancestors was won by those services to her about which none but initiates may hear; and she gave us two supreme gifts, grain and the holy rite, which brings its initiates more joyful hopes about the end of life and eternity.

[Isocrates, *Panegyricus* 4.28]

The emphasis of the Eleusinian rites was on individual participation and salvation. Alone among Athenian gods, Demeter gave hope of life after death:

How thrice-blessed are those who pass to Hades after seeing these mysteries; for only to them is it given to have life there, but to others all is evil there.   [Sophocles, Dindorf frg. 719]

Any Greek-speaker could be initiated into the Mysteries as long as they were properly introduced. Everyone believed in the power of the Mysteries and regarded them with the utmost respect. When a group of young aristocrats was suspected of parodying the rites in 415 BC, a furious investigation began.

A truce was declared 55 days before the Mysteries so that people could travel safely to the festival. They brought gifts of first fruits. Young men escorted priestesses with sacred objects in boxes the 14

44

miles from Eleusis to Athens. The Mysteries were a closely guarded secret: we do not know what these objects were.

The initiates gathered at the Painted Stoa and paid a fee. The next day they bathed themselves and a sacrificial piglet each in the sea for purification. One over-eager worshipper in the fourth century cut his piglet too soon and was attacked by a shark!

Two days later, after a quiet day indoors, they went in a procession with the sacred objects back to Eleusis. They wore garlands of myrtle and carried branches tied with wool, as well as bedding and clothes tied on a pole.

At the head of the procession rode the wooden statue of Iakkhos, called after the initiates' cry of 'Iakkhe! Iakkhe!' When the procession reached the bridge over the river Kephisos, hooded men met them shouting insults. These were intended to avert bad luck.

The procession reached Eleusis by torch light and the night was spent singing and dancing. The next day sacrifices of ground wheat were offered. In the evening the initiates drank the *kykeon*, a potion of meal, water and the herb pennyroyal. In their best clothes they entered the Telesterion, a square building surrounded by columns. Up to 10 000 people could attend the ceremony.

The Hierophantes, the 'revealer of holy things', a priest who always came from the same family, began a series of revelations in brilliant light. They consisted of 'things said', 'things done' and 'things shown', and may have included an enactment of the loss and recovery of Kore from the underworld by Demeter.

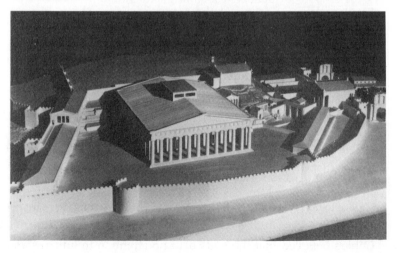

Model of the Telesterion at Eleusis

Only initiates called *epoptai* (viewers) were allowed to see the 'things shown'. We know little about what was seen. The early Christians made fun of the rites:

The Athenians celebrating the Eleusinian mysteries displayed to the initiates the great and wonderful and most mystic revelation of all – a harvested ear of corn.   [Hippolytos, *Refutation of Heresies* 5.8.39]

Nevertheless, the initiates certainly underwent a powerful emotional experience at Eleusis. It gave them a sense of personal involvement and a hope of some kind of salvation which was missing from other types of worship.

Blessed among men on earth is he who has seen these things. But he who is uninitiate in the holy rites, who has no lot in them, does not enjoy a like fate when he lies in death beneath broad-spreading darkness.
[Homeric hymn to Demeter, 479–82]

Critics

It is unlikely that there were any atheists in Athens. This did not mean, however, that everyone agreed about the extent of divine influence or that they did not criticise or even reject some beliefs and practices. The historian Thucydides, for example, provided natural rather than supernatural explanations for such things as eclipses, and was sceptical about oracles. He pointed out that during the plague of 430 BC, prayers to the gods were useless.

Similar ideas are found in the medical writers, in the plays of Euripides, and in the words of the sophists (teachers of 'wisdom' who offered a sort of higher education in Athens).

Some questioned the gods on moral grounds. This had begun with the sixth century thinker, Xenophanes:

Homer and Hesiod have attributed to the gods everything which is shameful and a reproach among men, stealing and committing adultery and deceiving each other.
[Xenophanes, Frg. 11 (quoted in Sextus *Adv. maths* ix, 193)]

The idea that the gods should be morally above reproach was taken up by Euripides:

I propose to you that if the gods do anything which is wrong, they are not gods.   [Euripides, *Bellerophon* frg. 292]

Others believed that the gods paid no attention to humans and required none in return:

Aristodemos said, 'I certainly don't despise the gods, Socrates; but I reckon them too high and mighty to need my attention.'

[Xenophon, *Memorabilia* 1.4.10]

Diagoras, the dithyrambic poet, was wronged by a man who broke his oath and got away with it, and he began saying that the gods did not exist. And Kritias, one of the Thirty Tyrants, said that the ancients invented God to act as a sort of supervisor of man's good and bad behaviour, so that fear of divine vengeance might discourage anyone from harming his neighbour secretly. [Sextus Empiricus, *Against the Teachers* 1.53]

The Thirty Tyrants were set over Athens by Sparta at the end of the Peloponnesian War. They were notorious for their murderous cruelty.

Others cast doubt on various aspects of religious belief, such as prophecy:

When Antiphon was asked what prophecy was, he said: 'A guess by a sensible man.' [Fragment 9]

or the supernatural origin of illness:

On the 'Sacred Disease' (epilepsy): this disease does not seem to me to be more sacred and divine than any other, but has its own nature and cause. Men's ignorance makes them regard it as sacred.

[Hippocrates, *Sacred Disease* 1]

The sophist Protagoras expressed a view we call agnosticism:

About the gods I am unable to know either that they exist, or that they do not; for there are many obstacles to knowledge, the obscurity of the subject and the brevity of human life. [Diogenes Laertius 9.51]

There is a story – unlikely to be true – that the Athenians burnt Protagoras' books in the agora.

Nevertheless, Greek religion continued because it was felt to work. The advance of science did not really affect people's beliefs, as this story of Plutarch's shows:

There is a story that Pericles was once sent the head of a one-horned ram from his country estate. Lampon, the *mantis*, saw that the horn grew strong and solid out of the middle of the ram's forehead and declared that the mastery of the two dominant parties in the city – which at that time were led by Thucydides [not the historian] and Pericles – would be concentrated in the hands of one man, the one who had received the portent. Anaxagoras, on the other hand, had the skull dissected and demonstrated that the brain had not filled its natural space, but had contracted into a point like an egg and extended only to that area where the root of the horn began.

On that occasion, it was Anaxagoras who won the admiration of the onlookers, but not long afterwards Lampon came into his own, for Thucydides was overthrown and the entire control of affairs came into Pericles' hands. [Plutarch, *Pericles* 6, 2–3]

Science did not have such an easy victory over religion!

5

Births, marriages and deaths

Giving birth

In spite of many misunderstandings of the female body, the famous doctor Hippocrates knew well enough the risk women faced in giving birth:

The birth is easy if the head comes first, but if the child comes sideways or feet first (this can happen ... if the mother has not kept still at the beginning of her birth-pangs) the birth is difficult and often fatal.

[Hippocrates, *The nature of the child* 30]

The pain and risks of childbirth were well known. A character in one of Euripides' tragedies aptly compares the significant moments in the lives of a man and a woman:

I would prefer to stand in the front rank of battle three times rather than give birth once.   [Euripides, *Medea* 250–1]

It seems from the sculpture shown overleaf that men were not present at the birth. The mother was helped by female midwives and other women.

There can be no doubt that many husbands were sympathetic and considerate to their wives:

The wife conceives and bears her burden. She suffers pains and endangers her life; she gives away the food which sustains her. She goes through a period of labour, gives birth and brings up her child with care. She has no reward in advance. She cares for the baby day and night laboriously for a long period, with no expectation of recompense.

[Socrates in Xenophon, *Memorabilia* 2.2.5]

The birth of a child increased the wife's status within the household:

When I decided to marry, gentlemen, I was generally disposed not to harass my wife or object to her doing what she wanted, but by the time my child was born, I already trusted her completely and I put all my property

49

at her disposal, thinking this the truest expression of the bond between us.   [Euphiletos in Lysias, *Eratosthenes* 6–10]

Exposure

The father decided whether to bring up the child. If it was weak or deformed, or if the *oikos* (household) could not afford another child, it was left outside the city, where it would either die or be rescued and enslaved. This gruesome custom was called exposure.

It is reasonable to assume that girls were more often exposed than boys, and that most of the exposed babies were the offspring not of well-off citizen women, but of slave-girls and prostitutes. Not surprisingly, we have no evidence for the numbers of children treated in this way.

A woman giving birth

Family celebrations

If the father decided to keep the baby, the door of the house was decorated with an olive branch for a boy and a piece of wool for a girl – an early reminder of her later work and her lower value. The women who had been present at the birth purified themselves by washing. One picked up the baby and carried it round the family fire, thus symbolically introducing it into the worship of the gods.

On the tenth day after the birth, there was a family feast and a sacrifice. The child was shown to relatives and friends and named by the father. From now until the child went to school at the age of seven (in the case of a boy), the responsibility for upbringing lay with the mother.

Children's festivals

A new stage of a male child's life was marked by his appearance at two festivals.

The Anthesteria

The name of this festival comes from the Greek word *anthos*, a flower. The first part of the celebrations were in honour of Dionysos, god of birth and growth and of the new wine. Three-year-old boys wore crowns of flowers and joined in the second day of the festival, which was called 'Wine-jugs'. Everyone received a measure of wine diluted with water, in a special jug. Amidst silence a bugle sounded and they began to drink. There was a prize for the first person to drain his jug.

Slaves and children took part in this competition. As the jugs given to adults held over two litres of wine, it is fortunate that children had smaller jugs, which they kept as presents. They had special scenes on them, usually of fat children playing.

The Apatouria

At the gathering of his father's clan or family association (*phratria*) in the autumn, the three-year-old boy was introduced. On the first day of the festival, the members of the *phratria*, who might live anywhere in Attica, had a meal together and caught up on the news. The second day was spent sacrificing and on the third, new members were introduced. The father would offer a sacrifice on behalf of his son, and the boy was registered with the *phratria*. The priest was entitled to a fee of half a drachma, and a thigh, side and ear of the sacrificial victim. The rest, with cakes and wine, was eaten with family and friends.

The father had to swear that he knew 'that the child had citizen status, being born to him from a citizen mother properly married' (Demosthenes 57.54). This was important in establishing the boy's rights to citizenship later.

Coming of age

At the age of sixteen, boys were considered to have come of age. On the third day of the Apatouria, they cut their hair to show that their childhood was over.

Two years later, the young men were registered with their deme (local community). They had first to prove their rights to be citizens, but this was probably no more than a formality. In cases of doubt, the *phratria* records could be referred to.

An Anthesteria jug

Epheboi

Young men between the ages of eighteen and twenty were known as *epheboi*. Most of their time was spent on military service on the frontiers of Attica. They also had an important part to play in some religious events, such as the Eleusinian Mysteries and the Pana-thenaia, which are described in Chapter 4.

In the fourth century, the *epheboi* were organised into a college and military service became compulsory. They swore an oath which may have existed earlier. It gives an insight into Athenian values:

1. I will not disgrace these sacred arms.
2. I will not desert my companions in battle.
3. I will defend our sacred and public institutions.
4. I will leave my fatherland better and greater, as far as I am able.
5. I will obey the magistrates and the laws and defend them against those who seek to destroy them.

Witnesses are the gods . . . and the boundaries of the fatherland.

At the age of twenty a young man was no longer an *ephebos*. He could attend the *ecclesia* and begin his life as a citizen.

Marriage

The purpose of marriage

We have wives to produce true-born children and to be trustworthy guardians of the household.   [Demosthenes 59.122]

The purpose of marriage was made quite clear in the betrothal formula spoken by the girl's father to the intended bridegroom:

I give you this woman for the ploughing of legitimate children.

The *oikos* (household) must be kept as a unit and handed on to blood relations. Therefore it was vital that Athenian girls should be virgins when they married.

Some men were suspicious of marriage:

For there is nothing better that a man can acquire than a good wife, but nothing worse than a bad one, who is greedy, who burns a man, no matter how strong he is, and makes him old before his time.

[Hesiod, *Works and Days* 700–3]

Others were openly cynical:

The two best days in a woman's life are when someone marries her and when her dead body is carried to the grave.

[Hipponax, a sixth century satirist]

It is impossible for us to know how Athenian girls felt about marriage. They were brought up with this as their goal, and might be betrothed as early as five. The betrothal was a contract between the girl's father and the bridegroom or his father, and this custom was accepted, as it is in some cultures today. Marriage was not based on love, and at that age girls had no choice.

Father, when I was a young girl, you had to find a husband to whom to give me. The choice was yours then.

[Fragment of comedy (4th or 3rd century)]

The character speaking here implies that an older bride might be expected to have a say in the choice of her husband.

Dowries

At the betrothal, the friends and relatives of both sides were present (though not necessarily the girl herself). They bore witness to the girl's virginity and to the size of the dowry.

The dowry was a sum of money, or property valued in cash, which was the share of the *oikos* estate set aside for girl children. It was used to support them while they were married and if they were divorced it had to be returned. The woman could never actually own it or dispose of it herself.

No *kyrios* (head of the household) failed to give a dowry if he could help it; he would even mortgage his property if necessary. Friends and relatives would step in to help poor fathers, and just occasionally the state intervened:

Aristeides did not leave enough money even to pay for his funeral. It is also said that the state paid for his daughters to be married from the Prytaneum [building for the Standing Committee] and voted 3000 drachmas outright to each daughter as a dowry. [Plutarch, *Aristeides* 27]

Weddings

A wedding was a private contract which became valid as the bride entered her husband's house. There was no need for a ceremony to register and legalise the marriage. Nevertheless, weddings were a time for celebration and there were many traditional customs.

The Athenians had ideas about the best time to get married.

Hesiod and the philosopher Aristotle both recommend the winter months.

The bride's *kyrios* sacrificed to the goddesses of marriage, Hera, Artemis and the Fates, and the bride dedicated a lock of her hair to them. Both the bride and groom bathed in water from the Kallirhoe (Beautifully-flowing) fountain at the foot of the Acropolis. Water was brought for the bride in a specially shaped jar called a *loutrophoros*. If a girl died before she could be married, one of these jars was placed on her grave.

Both bride and groom wore their best clothes. The bride was veiled and wore a headband. The doors of her father's house were hung with ivy and bay leaves. The bride was escorted to her new home by the bridegroom and a close friend or relative of his. She sat between them in a chariot drawn by mules or oxen. For a woman, this was one of her longest appearances in the streets; otherwise she might appear only for festivals, funerals and other people's weddings. During the procession, a wedding song was sung to the music of pipes. The couple received greetings and congratulations as they went along. This sort of procession often takes place in Mediterranean countries today.

The arrival of a bride at her new home

When the bride reached her new home, she found her mother-in-law waiting to greet her with a lighted torch. Nuts and fruit were showered on the couple, as sugared almonds are distributed at Italian weddings today. Next came the wedding feast. It was important to have a large number of guests to witness the contract. Women attended the feast but sat separately from the men, the bride still veiled among them.

When the eating and drinking were over, the husband led his wife to the bedroom. Another hymn, called an *epithalamion*, was sung outside the door. The bride and groom ate a quince together, perhaps as a symbol of fertility. This custom had been introduced by the sixth century law-maker, Solon. Plutarch says that it was supposed to ward off evil influences.

The next day, friends sent presents and the girl's married life began – and her education, if she had a husband like Ischomachos:

I implored the assistance of the gods, to show me what instructions were necessary for my new wife; and that she might have a heart to learn and practise these instructions to the advantage and profit of us both.   [Xenophon, *Oeconomicus* 7]

Ischomachos' wife was fifteen – about half his age.

Adultery

It was vital to the husband and the proper continuation of his *oikos* that the wife should be absolutely faithful. Adultery was dealt with severely.

Euphiletos was prosecuted for killing Eratosthenes, whom he caught in bed with his wife. Here he is speaking in his own defence:

A man who seduces a woman corrupts her and makes her closer to him than to her legal husband. He establishes an influence on the whole household and the husband cannot be sure whether the children are truly his own.   [Lysias 1.33]

This view would have made sense to the male jury, who for this reason no doubt shared Euphiletos' opinion that seduction was worse than rape!

It was also in the public interest that adultery should be prevented, for the state depended on the security of the individual *oikoi* which made it up.

When a man catches an adulterer, he shall not continue to live with his wife; if he does, he shall forfeit citizen rights.

[Law on adultery, Demosthenes 59.86]

Of course, a husband who had spent his wife's dowry might not be able to return her to her family so easily!

Contraception

Once a man and woman were married, it was expected that children would follow as soon as possible. Contraception was not unknown, but citizen wives had no need for it – luckily for them, if this example is anything to go by:

If a woman does not want to become pregnant, make as thick a mixture as possible of beans and water, make her drink it and she will not become pregnant for a year. [Hippocrates, *Nature of women* 98]

The advantages of pregnancy

The male view of women's health is summed up in the writings of Hippocrates, the famous doctor from the island of Kos, who wrote in about 430 BC.

Another point about women: if they have intercourse with men, their health is better than if they do not.

[Hippocrates, *Embryology and Anatomy* 4]

Pregnancy was even thought to be able to cure illnesses:

A woman for a long time had headaches, and no-one could help her at all, not even when she had her head drained. But when she became pregnant, her headaches disappeared. [Hippocrates, *Epidemics*, 5.12]

If the womb was not filled, it might start wandering about the body and causing all sorts of illnesses for which the cures were often even worse. For example:

If her womb moves towards her hips, her periods stop coming and pain develops in her lower stomach and abdomen. When this condition occurs, wash the woman with warm water, make her eat as much garlic as she can, and have her drink undiluted sheep's milk after her meals. Then fumigate her and give her a laxative. [Hippocrates, *Nature of women* 8.3]

This 'cure' was to be followed by a series of pessaries, but if even these failed, the poor woman had to drink four beetles with peony seeds, cuttlefish eggs and parsley seed in wine.

Death

The importance of burial

Funerals were the responsibility of the family, as they are today:

The person responsible shall lay out the corpse within the house as he thinks fit. He shall carry out the corpse the following morning before sunrise. [Law of Solon, quoted in Demosthenes 43.62]

Failure to bury a corpse was a disgrace to the dead and the living. After a sea battle in 406 BC, some of the generals did not go back to pick up the men and corpses in the sea. They were sentenced to death.

Anyone who saw a corpse was obliged by law to put earth on it. Three handfuls were enough to count as a burial. Exile was a dreaded punishment because, among other things, an exiled man could not be buried in his family ground – nor could he attend to his ancestors' tombs. When the Persians invaded Attica, the Athenian battle cry was:

Free your native land, free your children, wives, the shrines of your ancestral gods, and the tombs of your ancestors.
[Aeschylus, *Persians* 403–5]

It was only in times of great crisis, like the plague in 430 BC, that families failed to carry out their proper duties to the dead. Thucydides saw this as an indication of a breakdown of fundamental values:

All the funeral ceremonies which used to be observed were now disorganised, and they buried the dead as best they could. Many people adopted the most shameless methods. They would arrive first at a funeral pyre which had been made by others, put their own corpse on it and set it alight; or, finding another pyre burning, they would throw the corpse they were carrying on top of the other one and go away. [Thucydides 2.52.4]

Funerals

The main public cemetery in Athens was the Kerameikos, outside the Dipylon Gate. Burial inside the city boundaries was a rare honour, reserved for the bones of heroes like Theseus, the legendary founder of Athens:

The Athenians were overjoyed and welcomed Theseus' relics with magnificent processions and sacrifices, as though the hero himself were returning to the city. He lies buried in the heart of Athens, and his tomb is a

Loutrophoros showing a scene of mourning

sanctuary for runaway slaves and all who are poor and down-trodden, for Theseus all through his life was the champion of the distressed.

[Plutarch, *Life of Theseus* 36]

The Athenians practised burial and cremation. Cremation was more expensive because of the cost of the wood for the funeral pyre – the reverse of the situation in England today, where the cost of land makes burial more expensive.

The first stage was the *prothesis* (laying out) of the corpse. The women of the family washed the body, anointed it with perfumed oil, dressed it and put a garland of flowers round the neck. It was then placed on a bier (funeral bed) in the house, and friends and relatives were invited to visit.

A day of mourning usually took place, in spite of Solon's law that the funeral should be the day after the laying out. In fact, attempts by law to restrict shows of grief were doomed to failure. Women dressed in black, uttering shrill cries. Mourners were hired. They tore their hair, beat their breasts and scratched their cheeks. Relatives cut their hair, wore filthy clothing and poured ashes on their heads. You can see much the same in Greece today.

Death caused pollution, so anyone who came in contact with the corpse had to purify themselves. A bowl of water was placed outside the house for departing visitors and as a warning to others. As well as its religious significance, this custom had a sound sanitary basis.

The *ekphora* (carrying out) of the corpse was normally on the third day. The body was wrapped in a shroud and a cloak and carried in procession – on a wagon if the family could afford it – to the cemetery. If it was to be cremated, a pyre would have been built in advance. Once the corpse was burnt, it was the duty of the nearest relative to gather the bones from among the ashes.

A small coin was often put in the corpse's mouth to pay Charon, the ferryman who would take the dead person's spirit across the River Styx into the Underworld. We cannot be sure whether the Athenians believed literally in an Underworld ruled over by Hades, but they seem to have taken no chances; the dead person's most important possessions were buried with him or her in case there was need of them. In men's graves weapons and knives are often found, and jewellery, clothes and cloth-making equipment in women's.

Offerings of oil and wine were made at the side of the grave, and a funeral feast was held. On the third and ninth days after the funeral, food was again brought to the grave. The period of mourning lasted for 30 days, at the end of which the family and friends gathered to eat together.

Grave markers

A thin stone slab (*stele*) was the usual type of gravestone up to 435 BC. Until then, gravestones with figures were forbidden by law – in an attempt to limit obvious spending by rich families. After 435 BC, many beautiful sculptures appeared, and gravestones were wider and shorter to hold them. They showed the dead person as he or she had been in life. The name was given in an inscription.

Often, special jars of oil were left on graves. These jars, called *lekythoi*, had a white background. The scenes on them were usually connected with death, and they give us further evidence for graves and funeral customs. Many of them are drawn simply and feelingly.

The cult of the dead

The city held days of the dead (*nekysia*) and days of the forefathers (*genesia*). Drink offerings were poured on graves – barley broth, milk, honey, wine, oil and blood. It was believed that as the liquid seeped into the earth, contact was made with the dead and prayers could reach them.

Food was also offered and burnt at the graves. Sacrifices were held regularly to honour the dead – and feed the living.

The Anthesteria again

The Anthesteria was not only a children's festival to celebrate Dionysos' help in producing the new wine. The third day was called 'Pots', and it was a polluted day, when the dead walked.

People cooked pots of mixed vegetables and offered them to Hermes, the god who guided the souls of the dead to the Underworld. They also chewed buckthorn leaves first thing in the morning to keep ghosts away, and painted the doors of their houses with pitch. All the sanctuaries of the city were roped off. The Chinese have a similar day in modern times.

At the end of this frightening day, the Athenians shouted, 'Get out, Evil Spirits, the Anthesteria is over!'

A grave stele

6

Work and the economy

Attitudes to work

Xenophon, quoting Socrates, summed up the attitude of the upper-class citizens to work:

Jobs in craft and industry have a bad reputation and are regarded with contempt. For they ruin those who do them both physically and mentally. For those low-class jobs do not allow people enough time to be with their friends or to take any part in public life, with the result that such workers are obviously bad at social and political activities.

[Xenophon, *Oeconomicus* 4.2–3]

Finally, Socrates names agriculture and soldiery as the two professions least unsuitable for a free man. As Socrates' own father was a stonemason and his mother a midwife, we may assume that the view expressed here was Xenophon's own. Few could afford such an outlook. But those who could saw work as an infringement of a citizen's leisure and therefore of his ability to take part in the affairs of his city as he should. Aristotle also saw it as a hindrance to the development of virtue:

It follows that in the state which is best governed, ... the citizens must not lead the life of craftsmen or tradesmen, for such a life is ignoble ... Neither must they be farmers, since leisure is necessary both for the development of virtue and the performance of political duties. [Aristotle, *Politics* 7.8.2]

Nevertheless, the vast majority of the citizens of Athens relied on the land for a living, and many farmed themselves, with the help of slaves. Farmers engaged in the hard round of sowing, harvesting and ploughing could hardly hold a contemptuous view of their work. Hesiod, the farmer-poet, put the opposite view:

It is from work that men are rich in flocks and wealthy, and a working man is much dearer to the gods. Work is no reproach, but not working *is* a reproach. [Hesiod, *Works and Days* 308–10]

Work in the country

As we saw in Chapter 1, Attica was rich in natural resources. The business of tapping them provided employment for many people. The clay had to be dug out and transported to the workshops in Athens; near the quarries were areas for stone cutting; and there were ore-washing workshops near the mines which gave off toxic fumes and added to the miseries of the workforce. It is likely that even in the dark, narrow and dangerous passages of the mines – they were only one metre square – a few citizens worked alongside the slaves. At Acharnai, charcoal was certainly made by citizens as well as slaves. Charcoal burning is a difficult job which to this day in the Mediterranean region is passed on from father to son.

Manufacture

The Athenians had nothing like industry on a modern scale. They had no factories as we know them today and made almost no technological advances – this has sometimes been ascribed to the fact that slave labour was so cheap and readily available.

It is realistic to refer to 'workshops' rather than factories. The largest we know of was owned by the metic Cephalos and employed 120 slaves. They made armour. The orator Demosthenes was the son of a man who had one workshop with 32 knife-makers and another with 20 carpenters making beds, but these too were exceptionally large. Even Timarchos' 9 shoemakers and a foreman were noteworthy. The usual number of men working together was probably five or six. Citizens, metics and slaves worked side by side.

Skilled workers earned a drachma a day, the same wage as soldiers and sailors on campaign. Unskilled workers (and jurymen) were paid three obols (half a drachma).

The working day began early in Athens, as it tends to in hot countries:

When the cock sings his dawn song, up they all jump and rush off to work, the bronze-smiths, the potters, the tanners, the shoemakers, the bath-attendants, the corn-merchants, the lyre-shapers and the shield-makers, and some of them even put on their sandals and leave when it's still dark.   [Aristophanes, *Birds* 489–92]

These trades had their own areas near the agora, such as the Cerameikos or Potters' Quarter. Pottery was one of the largest-

A shoemaker gives a fitting

scale manufactures in Athens and was, along with silver, oil and wine, one of the main exports.

Commerce

The commercial life of Athens centred on the Peiraieus, an international port and clearing house by the fifth century. The thousands of visitors who came and went there every year – whether for trade or tourism – made an important contribution to the economy.

The city established Peiraieus as a trading centre in the middle of Greece, of such magnitude that individual items which are difficult to obtain from different individual sources can all be provided with ease from there.

[Isocrates, *Panegyricus*, 4.42]

There were two harbours at the Peiraieus for the ships of the Athenian fleet. Service in the navy offered employment to poorer citizens. They also found work at the docks of the Kantharos harbour, unloading the vast number of goods necessary for survival – and for civilised life: wheat, iron, tin, copper, timber, slaves, ivory, semi-precious stones, hides, leather, flax, papyrus and many more.

The greatness of our city means that all the things from all over the world flow in to us, so that it seems just as natural to enjoy foreign goods as our own local products. [Thucydides 2.38.2]

The poet Hermippos reflects the Athenians' pride in their ability to import from all over the Mediterranean area:

From Cyrene we have silphium and ox-hide, from the Hellespont fresh and dried fish, from Italy come grains of wheat and sides of beef. Syracuse provides pigs and cheese, from Egypt come sails and papyrus and from Syria frankincense. Beautiful Crete provides cypress-wood, while Libya sends quantities of ivory. Rhodes obliges with raisins and figs which bring on sweet dreams. From Euboea come pears and big, juicy apples and from Phrygia slaves. The Paphlagonians send chestnuts and almonds, Phoenicia grows dates for us and makes a fine wheat flour; Carthage provides carpets and embroidered cushions. [Athenaeus 1.27d–g]

Shipbuilding and the small-scale manufacture of Athens – of fabrics, weapons, kitchen ware, jewellery, furniture and leather – depended on imported raw materials. There were few exports to balance the enormous import bill. Athens relied on the 'invisible exports' of trade and tourism and the income from her empire to balance the books.

The grain trade

You know that we are more dependent than anyone else on imported grain. Most of our supplies come from the Black Sea.

[Demosthenes, *Against Leptines* 20. 30–3]

As we saw in Chapter 1, most Athenian farmers grew barley rather than wheat, and not enough of that to feed the population. There have been various calculations of the extent of the shortfall. One estimate is that home-produced grain could feed only about 75000 out of a possible total population of 300000.

Athens relied on the rich wheatfields of the Ukraine and Crimea. Her surrender in the Peloponnesian War in 404 BC was due less to a military defeat than to the fact that Sparta had finally succeeded in cutting off the grain route.

The importance of the grain trade was marked by the fact that it

An Athenian silver drachma with Athene's owl

was treated separately for tax purposes and overseen by a special board of grain commissioners.

Money-lending

Athenian citizens did not often take part in long-distance, overseas trade, but they might own ships or make loans of up to 2000 drachmas to finance people daring enough to purchase a cargo and risk a voyage.

Some distinguished between 'idle' and 'working' capital and saw the value of money-lending:

It is not the borrowers but the lenders who are responsible for the prosperity of all sea trade. [Demosthenes, *Against Phormion* 51]

The philosophers disapproved, however:

The most hated sort of trade – and with the greatest reason – is usury, which makes a gain out of money itself. For money was intended to be used in exchange, but not to increase at interest. [Aristotle, *Politics* 1.3.23]

Retail trade

Local retail traders were almost all citizens or metics. Shopping was normally done by men, and it was rather like going to an open market or fair today. People sold their goods from the workshops attached to houses, in the stoa on the road between the agora and the Dipylon Gate and in the agora itself from booths, tables or round platforms on which could be displayed meat, fish, fabrics, leather, pots or slaves.

Xenophon tells us that slaves sent to the agora to do the shopping could make no mistake, for everything had its own place – garlic, onions, frankincense, perfume and so on. Barbers and fishmongers were to be found on the north side of the agora. Here too were the bankers. The ancient Greek word for a table, *trapeza*, is the modern word for a bank. The services offered ranged from money-changing to lending at interest (usually 12%) and insurance. The bankers were usually metics.

Olive oil was sold on the east side of the agora – vital for preserving food and cooking, lighting, and use on the skin. Books, which were papyrus scrolls, were sold in the centre of the agora in an area called the orchestra, probably where the dramatic contests had taken place before they moved to the theatre of Dionysos.

Not all citizens could afford to keep their wives at home. Women who worked in the retail trade had their own area in the agora.

They sold such things as vegetables and garlands and ribbons for sacrifices. The tragic poet Euripides was constantly mocked on the grounds that his mother sold herbs in the agora:

Euripides, my dearest, sweetest Euripides, give me some chervil, borrowed from your mother.   [Dikaiopolis in Aristophanes, *Acharnians* 477]

Women also worked in the bars.

The activities of the agora were supervised by ten Controllers of Measures, chosen annually by lot, to ensure standards in weights and measures, and ten Market Officials, who made sure that the produce sold was pure and genuine – that, for example, the fishmongers were not soaking their fish in water to add to its weight and give a false impression of freshness.

A fishmonger supplies a customer

Taxation

Metics paid tax; Athenian citizens did not. They would have regarded any direct tax as intolerable. However, there were compulsory duties to the state for both citizens and metics who owned over a fixed amount of wealth.

The proper performance of these expensive duties brought great credit, and some men, like Lysias the speech-writer in the fourth century, chose to expend far more than they had to. These duties were called liturgies, and emergency war taxes were *eisphorai*.

They could be a burden. Socrates is speaking here:

I see that the state already imposes considerable obligations on you, making you pay for the keeping of horses, the training of choruses and gymnastic teams, and putting you in charge of other operations; what is more, if a war breaks out, I know that they will demand from you trierarchies and *eisphorai* of a size you will find difficult to manage. [Xenophon, *Oeconomicus* 2.6]

A trierarchy was the duty of keeping a state trireme in good order for a year, providing, though not feeding, a crew, and either commanding it in person or finding a suitable person to do so.

Other liturgies were concerned with festivals. They included selecting, financing and training a team or chorus for the athletic, musical or dramatic contests; paying the expenses of a delegation to a non-Athenian festival, such as the Olympic Games; and providing a feast for a tribe.

The only way to avoid a liturgy was to find someone who appeared to be richer, yet doing less, and challenge him either to do the liturgy instead or to exchange property. But most upper-class citizens were eager to win praise through conspicuous expenditure:

'What I enjoy is honouring the gods on a generous scale, helping my friends if they need anything and seeing that the city does not go unadorned for lack of money so far as I can.' [Ischomachos in Xenophon, *Oeconomicus* 11.9]

Some wealthy American families – the Carnegies, Leverhulmes and Gettys – inherited a similar attitude. The Athenian state was successful in handing over major expenditure to individuals – most of whom were grateful for the opportunity to contribute.

7

Entertainment

The festivals provided the Athenians with holidays throughout the year. Thousands gathered to join in the processions and competitions, or simply to watch. When everyone else went back to work, the rich remained at leisure.

It is not possible for everyone to do the same work, because of differences in circumstances. Our ancestors therefore decided that the less well-off should farm and trade, while those who had private means should spend their time on riding, athletics, hunting and philosophy.

[Isocrates, *Areopagiticus* 44–5]

Hunting and fishing

For most countrymen, hunting and fishing were for food, not sport, as this dedication suggests:

Three brothers dedicate to Pan these implements of their trade: Damis gives the net he uses for animals of the mountains; Kleitor gives this fishing net and Pigres offers this net ... which entangles birds by their necks. Their home never saw them returning with empty nets.

[Greek Anthology 6.14 Antipater of Sidon]

The gods naturally came first in sport as in every other aspect of life:

Games and hounds are an invention of the gods Apollo and Artemis.   [Xenophon, *On hunting* 1]

Xenophon recommends hunting as a valuable training for war and to build a noble character. Plato could not see the same advantages in fishing:

In contests with sea bass or conger eels or parrot fish, there is no display of bravery or examples of strength, speed or agility.

[Plato, *Laws* 823E quoted by Plutarch, *On the cleverness of animals*, 9]

But some centuries later, the poet Oppian expressed the eternal joys of fishing:

What pleasure the fisherman has when he pierces the jaw of his prey with hook of bronze, and sweeps the twisting dancer from the depths high into the air! [Oppian, *On hunting* 1.47–66]

The fisherman's equipment consisted of a rod, with a bent hook of horn or bronze, a net with lead weights, traps and tridents. He might fish from a boat or simply from the rocks. Larger fish like the tuna and swordfish were hunted, as they still are, by harpooners.

The huntsman took no chances. He hunted on foot and his chief prey were hares, deer and wild boars. Dogs drove the hares into nets and the huntsman dispatched them with a club. Roe deer were also caught in nets, and by snares in the form of a wooden clog which caught the hoof and prevented the deer from running. Xenophon recommends using a captured fawn to lure its mother into the open; she could then be attacked with dogs and javelins. The dangerous wild boar, still hunted in Italy today, required a

A hunter and his dog

71

party of men with Spartan hounds, nets, spears and javelins.

Farmers must have been relieved that huntsmen were given this advice:

It is advisable to take the hounds to the mountains often, but less frequently to cultivated land.   [Xenophon, *On hunting* 4.9]

Conversation

The Athenians have always loved talking. Here the speaker is defending the men who came to his shop against a charge of 'loitering with intent':

Everyone of you frequents the scent-shop, the barber's or the saddler's or whatever . . . so if any of you has any criticism of those who come into my premises, the same criticism is valid against those who frequent the other shops – and that means the whole population of Athens, for you all like lounging and gossiping here, there and everywhere.   [Lysias 24.20]

St Paul found things no different in the first century AD:

Now all the Athenians and the foreigners who lived there spent their time in nothing except telling or hearing something new.
                    [Acts of the Apostles 17.21]

A scene in the palaistra

72

Athletics

Among the favourite meeting places were the gymnasia or training grounds (from the Greek word *gymnos,* naked, for the Greeks took their clothes off for exercise). There were three gymnasia in and around Athens, the Lykeion, the Academy and Cynosarges. All were sacred groves beside a stream.

Plato, who set up his school of philosophy in the Academy, describes a typical scene there:

When we went in, we found that the boys had finished the sacrifices, and had pretty well completed the religious business and were playing knucklebones in their best clothes. Most of them were playing in the open air in the courtyard, but some were in a corner of the dressing room playing at odds-and-evens.   [Plato, *Lysis* 206e–7a]

The main feature of a gymnasium was its running track, but most also contained a *palaistra* or wrestling ground. There were jumping pits and areas for discus and javelin practice. The buildings included bathrooms and an oil-store and a dust-room, for athletes used to rub olive oil on their bodies and dust themselves lightly before wrestling or the pankration (a violent mixture of boxing and wrestling).

Physical training was a very important part of Greek education, and fitness was part of the Athenian ideal. This could be explained on military grounds – the Athenian hoplites had to be fit – but it was also valued for its own sake:

People with bodies in good condition are healthy and strong: they are able to save their lives honourably from the dangers of war and escape all disasters; many of them help their friends and serve their country, thereby winning thanks, glory and the highest honours.

[Xenophon, *Memorabilia* 3.12.4]

The elderly (and overweight) Socrates thought of taking lessons from an acrobatic dancer. When his friends teased him, he replied:

Are you laughing at me because I want to improve my health, my appetite and my sleeping by exercises of this kind? [Xenophon, *Symposion* 2.17]

We can compare the attitude of the Romans:

Hardly anyone dances except drunks – or madmen.

[Cicero, *For Murena* 13]

and the modern American:

Tough Guys Don't Dance. [Norman Mailer]

Under the supervision of their *paidotribes* (trainer), boys learnt to run, to long-jump with weights in their hands, to throw the discus and javelin and to wrestle. These were the events which made up the pentathlon. They were also trained in boxing, their fists bound with strips of leather. The results could be disastrous:

This man Olympikos, as he now appears, used to have a nose, chin, forehead, ears and eyelids. But then he enrolled in the Guild of Boxers... [Lucilius, Greek Anthology 11.75]

Every boy must have dreamt of a victory in one of the great 'crown games' at Olympia, Delphi, Corinth or Nemea, bringing glory on himself and his city. Even if he did not get that far, he could still hope to win a prize in the festival competition in Athens.

The most popular and exciting events at any games were the horse and chariot races. They were open only to the wealthy upper classes, as pasture land for horses was in short supply.

My father Alcibiades was not inferior to anyone in natural ability and strength, but he considered the athletic contests to be beneath him, for he knew that some of the athletes were of low birth, from small cities, and not well-educated. Consequently, he turned his attention to raising race-horses, an activity only possible for the most wealthy.

[Speech written for the young Alcibiades by Isocrates, *Team of horses* 33]

A lone voice

Amidst a general admiration for athletes and athletics, a character from one of Euripides' tragedies disagrees:

There are ten thousand things wrong with Greece, but none is worse than the athletes. For how does it benefit the city if a man wins a prize for wrestling or running fast or throwing the discus or artistically smashing someone's jaw?   [*Autolycus* (Dindorf frg. 282)]

Games

At the gymnasium Plato saw boys playing knucklebones and odds-and-evens, where one player hid a number of objects in one hand and his opponent had to guess whether he held an odd or even number. This rather boring game was often enlivened by betting. It depended on speed, like the modern Mediterranean game of 'morra', where one player brings out his hand from behind his back and the group guesses and shouts out the number of fingers he has extended.

Most non-athletic games were simple. The Athenians threw dice and had a board game called *pessoi*, something like draughts. Children played with hoops, stilts and yo-yos. Some adult games involved birds:

A four-horse chariot race

After the Persian Wars, the Athenians began the custom of holding cock-fights in the theatre once a year. [Aelian, *Varied History* 2.28]

Slightly less cruel was the odd game of 'quail-flicking':

One person would set the quail up; then the other would flick it with his forefinger, or pluck out the feathers from its head. If the quail stayed still, victory went to the person who had bred it; if it failed to do so and tried to escape, the flicker or plucker won. [Pollux, 9.107]

Dinner parties

As we saw in Chapter 2, the *andron* (men's room) was designed mainly for the purpose of holding dinners and drinking parties (*symposia*). Couches were arranged around the edges of the room for the men to recline on. The place of honour was to the right of the door. Men wore loose-fitting robes which, if we can judge by the paintings on pottery, tended to slip off as the evening wore on! They also wore garlands on their heads and perfume on their bodies.

Small rectangular tables for the food stood by each couch. When the serious drinking began they were removed. As always, the gods came first. Offerings of wine were made and a hymn was sung.

Wine was always diluted with water, as it was very powerful. Herbs were sometimes added:

The following ingredients are put into before-dinner drinks: pepper, salad leaves, myrrh, sedge and Egyptian perfume.

[Athenaeus, *Sophists at dinner* 2.66C]

Not everyone drank to get drunk. Three bowls only were recommended for health, pleasure and sleep. Any more could lead to 'uproar, black eyes and throwing the furniture'. Perhaps not surprisingly, there was a drain to the street to take away the spilt wine – and worse!

Musical entertainment was usually provided. *Aulos*-girls played the pipe. Dancers and acrobats might be employed for the evening:

After this, a hoop was brought in, bristling with sharp swords. The dancer did somersaults in and out through these, until the spectators were terrified that she might hurt herself, but she coolly completed her performance without accident.   [Xenophon, *Symposion* 2,II]

This could be compared with the sword-dance in the Scottish highlands. Much of the entertainment was created by the guests themselves, and great was the embarrassment if anyone could not take part.

So the well-educated man should be able both to sing and to dance well.   [Plato, *Laws* 654B]

The general Themistocles may have saved Athens in the Persian Wars, but he was looked down on because he was unable to play the lyre.

Music and singing were a vital part of an upper-class boy's education and were a feature of most religious occasions. Boys learnt to play the lyre, an instrument with seven strings of different pitch, its more elaborate form, the kithara, and the *aulos*, something like a modern oboe or clarinet – though fashions could change:

At school, Alcibiades was usually obedient to his teachers, but he refused to play the *aulos*, which he said distorted his features and prevented singing. Word soon got round about this, and the *aulos* was dropped altogether from a gentleman's education and came to be utterly despised.   [Plutarch, *Alcibiades* 2.4–6]

There were well-known drinking songs to be sung to the lyre, often concerning politics. Guests took turns to perform. Most difficult of all were the *skolia*: one guest held a myrtle branch and began with a short verse in any metre he chose; he then handed the branch to the next man who had to cap his verse with another, and so on round the room.

Plato wrote a *Symposion* in which Socrates and his friends discussed the nature of love. We do not know whether he was describing a real occasion, but the conversation must often have been on serious philosophical and political topics. Others preferred jokes, riddles and fables, or just gossip. Some played a game called *kottabos* with their left-over wine. There were several different ways of playing this game. Some people simply flicked wine at a target; others tried to sink a saucer floating on water. Other guests preferred to make sexual advances to the slaves, of either sex.

Drama

Twice a year, at the festivals of the Lenaia in January and the City Dionysia in March, plays were performed in the theatre of Dionysos at the foot of the Acropolis.

The festivals

The Lenaia was attended by citizens only, but the City Dionysia was an occasion to impress the world with the greatness of Athens. The ancient wooden statue of Dionysos was taken to the Academy and brought back in procession to his sanctuary by the theatre. There was another great procession with bulls for sacrifice and *phalloi*, Dionysos' fertility symbol. Grapes, wine in leather bottles and special loaves were offered to the god. After the sacrifice, everyone had a good dinner of beef and plenty of wine, and the night was spent in a *komos* (revel) with torch-lit singing and dancing in the streets.

The plays

Four days of the festival were spent in the theatre. The plays were in competition with each other, and at the end of the performances

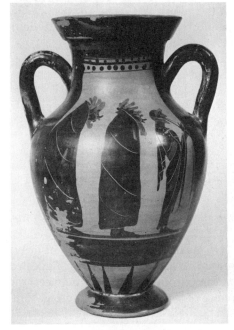

An 'aulos'-player and members of the chorus in a comedy

the ten judges awarded prizes. These brought great honour to the financial backer (the *choregos*), the playwright and the leading actor. Strict precautions were taken to avoid bribery.

Up to 17000 people could attend, and the theatre was always packed. The little evidence available suggests that women were allowed to be present at the tragedies, if not the comedies. The cost was 2 obols, but Pericles set up a fund for tickets for poorer citizens.

Tragedies

Tragedies had a chorus and no more than three individual actors who divided the parts among them. This was made easier by the fact that all performers wore masks. The chorus sang and danced but also took part in the action of the play.

The themes of tragedies were not always tragic in our sense. They almost always came from mythology – stories of gods and heroic men and women of the legendary past. They were often concerned with conflict, power, attitudes to the gods and the questioning of accepted values. The same story might be treated by different playwrights in different ways. For example, the three most successful poets of the fifth century, Aeschylus, Sophocles and Euripides, all dealt with the return of Orestes to avenge the murder of his father, Agamemnon, by killing his mother, Clytemnestra, and the consequences.

The interest for the audience lay in the way the poet chose to adapt and interpret the story and characters and the issues they chose to examine. The tragedies were powerful theatrical experiences and they made great demands on the audience, both intellectually and emotionally.

Satyr plays

Satyrs were half-animal creatures, companions of Dionysos. Each tragic poet had to write a satyr play to be performed after his three tragedies.

Only one satyr play survives in full, Euripides' *Cyclops*, but we know that the chorus dressed up as satyrs. It has been suggested that the effect of these plays came from the contrast between the down-to-earth, rowdy behaviour of the satyrs and the heroic world of tragedy.

Comedies

Aristophanes is the only comic poet whose plays have survived in more than fragments. Unlike tragedy, comedy dealt with contemporary life – although a fantastic and distorted view of it. The humour was slapstick and often obscene, and the chorus and actors attacked anything and anyone (with a few notable exceptions, such as the Eleusinian Mysteries). It is generally thought that one comedy was performed at the end of each day of tragedies. If so, the contrast must have been extraordinary.

Actors in comedy wore padded costumes, masks which were grotesque but sometimes recognisable, and a leather *phallos*. There were traditional routines and characters, as in pantomime today. All comedies included at least one *parabasis*, when the chorus came forward to offer more or less serious advice to the audience on political issues, and an *exodos* or finale, which usually involved a wedding or celebration – and often strong hints to the judges to award the play the prize.

Conclusion

Change and development

In a book of this length it is hard to avoid offering an over-simplified view of Athenian society. Above all, the impression may easily be given that life and attitudes remained much the same for everyone throughout the fifth century. This is far from being the case. We have only to consider the changes in Britain since Victorian times to realise how great a difference one hundred years can make, and Athens in the fifth century BC was in its own way changing as rapidly as twentieth century Britain.

Naturally, some attitudes – particularly concerning religious practices and the maintenance of the household – changed only very slowly or not at all. But in other fields – art, architecture and sculpture, and above all politics – there was continuous and radical change.

Political leadership

I maintain that it is appropriate that in Athens the poor and the common people should seem to have more power than the noble and rich, because it is this class that provides the rowers for the fleet and on which the power of the city is based. ['The Old Oligarch', *Constitution of Athens* I.I]

The fact that the city relied on the fleet and the fleet relied on them had not escaped the lowest class. There are signs of their increasing self-confidence and power; one of these is the change in the style of political leader elected after the death of Pericles. Thucydides disapproved:

But Pericles' successors, who were more on a level with each other and each of whom aimed at occupying the first place, adopted methods of demagogy which resulted in their losing control over the actual conduct of affairs. [Thucydides, 2.66]

Thucydides' own political prejudices led him to suggest that demagogy, which simply means 'leading the people', was nearer to rabble-rousing. He was wrong to blame this new style of leadership for Athens' defeat in the Peloponnesian War. But the lower classes were able to assert themselves without the sort of revolution which was so common in other Greek *poleis*, and this must have been due to the fact that all citizens, of whatever class, felt a shared commitment to their city.

Pride in the city

The fifth century Athenians were committed to their *polis*:

They devote their bodies to the community as though they were not their own, and they devote their minds, which are most truly their own, to achievement on its behalf. [Thucydides 1.70.6]

Pericles encouraged the citizens' recognition of their collective and individual achievement in the Funeral Speech:

Taking everything together, then, I declare that our city is an education to Greece, and I declare that in my opinion each single one of our citizens, in all the many aspects of life, is able to show himself the rightful lord and owner of his own person, and to do this, moreover, with exceptional grace and versatility. [Thucydides 2.41.1]

As the Athenians have not been the only society in the course of history to show a certain smugness – and many have had less reason – perhaps they can be forgiven this rather chauvinistic attitude:

So Plato [the story is also told of Socrates and others] gave thanks to nature, first that he was born a human being rather than a dumb animal; second that he was a man rather than a woman; then that he was a Greek not a foreigner; finally that he was Athenian born in the time of Socrates. [Lactantius, *Divine Institutions* 3.19]

Index